Rock Facts

Rock and Roll Hall of Fame and Museum

of

Fame

and

Museum

R

F

Ra

Rock and Roll Hall

Universe

Edited by James Henke

Text written by Steve Futterman, Billy Altman, and Parke Puterbaugh
Edited by James Henke and Erin Hogan

Some of the quotes appearing in the "If You Call It Music" section were previously published in Linda Martin and Kerry Seagrave, *Anti-Rock: The Opposition to Rock and Roll* (New York: Da Capo Press, 1993).

Photo Credits:
All photographs copyright © the individuals or agencies below.
Pages 26 (top), 70, 73, 76 (left and bottom right), 77 (all), 78 (background), 79 (top right), 80 (top), 81 (center and bottom), 82, 83 (all): Archive Photos.
Pages 38, 39, 41, 48, 49, 50: The Rock and Roll Hall of Fame and Museum/Andrew Moore.
Pages 40, 42–43, 45, 46–47: The Rock and Roll Hall of Fame and Museum/Tony Festa.
Page 68: Jay Blakesberg.
Page 95: Courtesy *Rolling Stone* magazine.
Pages 24, 26 (bottom), 76 (top right), 79 (top left): Archive Photos/Frank Driggs Collection.
Page 78 (inset): Globe Photos
Page 80 (bottom): The Image Works.
Page 81 (top): Retna/Camera Press Ltd.

Printed in Singapore
Design by Pentagram

For Rock and Roll Hall of Fame and Museum membership information, please call 1.800.349.ROCK. / First published in the United States of America in 1996 by UNIVERSE PUBLISHING / A Division of Rizzoli International Publications, Inc. / 300 Park Avenue South, New York, NY 10010 / Copyright © 1996 The Rock and Roll Hall of Fame and Museum, Inc. / All rights reserved. No part of this publication may be reproduced, stored in a retrieval system, or transmitted in any form or by any means, electronic, mechanical, photocopying, recording, or otherwise, without prior consent of the publishers.
/ 96 97 98 99 00 / 10 9 8 7 6 5 4 3 2 1

Library of Congress Cataloging-in-Publication Data

Rock facts / The Rock and Roll Hall of Fame and Museum ; with a foreword by James Henke.
p. cm.
ISBN 0-7893-0034-6 (hardcover)
1. Rock music—History and criticism. 2. Rock music—Miscellanea. 3. Rock musicians—Miscellanea. I. Rock and Roll Hall of Fame and Museum.
ML3534.R632 1996
781.66'09—dc20   96-17695
CIP
MN

After nearly a decade of planning, the Rock and Roll Hall of Fame and Museum opened its doors in September 1995. The Museum grew out of the Rock and Roll Hall of Fame Foundation, which was established in 1983 by members of the music industry to honor and recognize the artists, composers, producers and others who helped make rock and roll the most popular and influential art form of the second half of the twentieth century. Designed by renowned architect I. M. Pei and located on the shore of Lake Erie in downtown Cleveland, the Museum features an extensive collection of historic artifacts, ranging from rhythm & blues great Louis Jordan's saxophone to blues giant Muddy Waters's Fender Telecaster guitar to John Lennon's Sgt. Pepper uniform. By combining those artifacts with the latest technology—films, video walls, interactive computers—the Museum tells the story of rock and roll, from its roots in the blues, country, jazz and folk, through its birth in the fifties, its explosion in the sixties, and on to the present. From the start, it was our goal that the Museum not only pay tribute to the mega-stars of the sixties and seventies. Rather, we thought it crucial that we document the lesser-known artists who played key roles in the evolution of the music and, on the other end of the spectrum, that we deal with the music of today. To that end, the Museum visitor can see exhibits on a wide range of artists. The Everly Brothers and Elvis, Janis Joplin and the Supremes, U2 and Soundgarden are all represented in the Museum's exhibits. So are the Coasters and Ruth Brown, Grace Slick and the Rolling Stones, Run-D.M.C. and Nine Inch Nails. As we reach the end of this century, rock and roll has truly become a universal language, and the term rock and roll no longer describes just a style of music. Indeed, rock and roll encompasses everything from doo-wop to heavy metal, from rhythm & blues to rap. Beyond that, though, rock and roll also refers to an attitude, a feeling, a style, a way of life, and the Rock and Roll Hall of Fame and Museum's mission is to preserve both the history of the music, as well as that spirit.

"I like rock and roll, man; I don't like much else
There is nothing conceptually better tha
or Stones, has ever improved on 'Whol

Tell it like it is!

"That's the music that inspired me to play music. Rock and roll. No group, be it Beatles, Dylan, gotta Shakin'' for my money."—John Lennon

What is Rock?

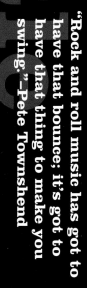

"'T' & 'b' stand for real black." —Little Richard

"Rock and roll motivates. It's the big, gigantic motivator." —Bruce Springsteen

"Rock and roll music has got to have that bounce; it's got to have that thing to make you swing."—Pete Townshend

"It's nothing but rhythm and blues. That's it."

"Rock and roll is fun, it's full of energy, it's full of laughter. It's naughty."–Tina Turner

"Mystery and mischief are the two most important ingredients in rock and roll."–Bono

"I mean wher
rock and roll w
thing, and we
scious that w
a new era. T
almost A.D. ar
was Year One,
world was b
and then sudd
living color."–

I was fifteen,

as a brand new

ere very con-

were in, like,

tally. It was

B.C., and 1956

ou know? The

ck-and-white

ly it went into

Keith Richards

"**Rhythm
is someth
you eithe
or don't h
but when
have it, y
it all over
Elvis Pre**

"Rock and roll is simply an
attitude. You don't have to play
the greatest guitar."–Johnny
Thunders

"You're not gonna beat rock and
roll music, and if you do, I want
to hear it."–Jerry Lee Lewis

ing

r have

ave,

you

u have

"

sley

"You're talking about music that was bred from Africa to the black church, the gospel, which turned into blues and jazz and country music. And if it cross-pollinates, that's the way it ought to be. That's the way it started." —Quincy Jones

"Rock and roll to me is communication. I don't just mean communication of ideas, but communication of feelings.... It's not necessarily that your idea is smart, but that it's your idea."
—The Edge "When you're singing and playing rock and roll, you're on the leading edge of yourself. You're trying to vibrate, trying to make something happen. It's like there's something alive and exposed." —Neil Young "It's a threat, really. I think that's really the key of it." –Suzanne Vega "It's the music that kept us all intact.... kept us from going crazy." –Lou Reed "Pure rock and roll is when the past no longer exists and the

future doesn't exist. It's like a flowing moment in the present when the band and the audience become as one and you occupy a moment completely and fully." –Joe Strummer "I was at the perfect age, puberty, when rock and roll hit me. It couldn't have been a more perfect sucker punch." –Robbie Robertson "Anyone who tells you they didn't get into rock and roll to get laid is lying." –Graham Nash "Rock and roll was something that's hardcore, rough and wild and sweaty and wet and just loose." –Patti Labelle "Let's face it, rock and roll is bigger than all of us." –Alan Freed

The Sounds of Silence: Before There Was Rock

America in the early fifties was a study in contrasts. Economic growth had opened new vistas of security and leisure time, all accompanied by a drab soundtrack of bloodless music. On the surface, with its tidy suburban lawns, Ozzie-and-Harriet media images and McCarthy-ish vigilance, the country was the picture of stability and order. A peek just below this veneer, however, revealed a bubbling brew of racial injustice, incipient adolescent rebellion and social unrest. Soon, rock and roll would sound that insurgent cry, but in the meantime, the dulcet—or just plain dull—sounds of Eddie Fisher, Patti Page and others of their rose-colored ilk filled the air. Where black society was grooving to the golden age of rhythm & blues, white America was still knee-deep in narcoleptic pop vocalists, Percy Faith schmaltz and—when it needed real subversive kicks—slightly naughty novelty hits like "Come On-A My House." In glorious flower everywhere were such indigenous regional musics as the blues, gospel, and country & western, but their sounds went unheard by the vast majority of Americans. Popular music of the time was drained of color and overt expressiveness, as if too much emotion and power might topple the house of cards.

Teenagers, flush with a forceful presence previously unknown in our nation's history, were left without a voice. With the airwaves saturated by the warbling of relentlessly chipper female vocalists and the steady-as-you-go pipings of male singers whose roots lay firmly in the swing era, it's little wonder sensation-starved teenagers desperately searched their radio bands for obscure stations that played the brave new music that spoke the true language of the city streets. Rock and roll was out there. . . . It just had to be found.

Robert Johnson
Jimmie Rodgers
Jimmy Yancey
Louis Jordan
T-Bone Walker
Hank Williams
Woody Guthrie
Lead Belly
Les Paul
The Ink Spots
Bessie Smith
The Soul Stirrers
Louis Armstrong
Charlie Christian
Ma Rainey
Howlin' Wolf
Elmore James
Professor Longhair
Dinah Washington
Willie Dixon
The Orioles
Pete Seeger

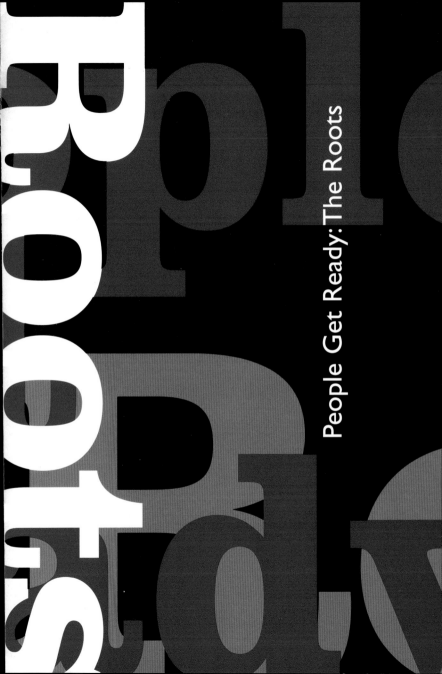

People Get Ready: The Roots

"Black people—they drew out of their community thi[s]
music and jazz and blues; and all those elements combine[d]
whites were attracted to it, it began to be known as roc[k]

The story of rock and roll is fundamentally no different from the story of American culture itself. Assimilation—the melding together of different ethnic, racial and regional strands—is central to the music that has come to define our country. Rock and roll speaks to so many Americans because it is extracted from so many different segments of American society and culture. It cuts across stylistic boundaries and social divisions. There would be no rock and roll without the roots music of African-American culture. Blues, gospel, rhythm & blues and jazz are rock and roll's essential foundations. The rhythms, song forms, instrumental expressiveness and vocal styles of rock and roll can almost all be found in these African-American musical genres. African slaves brought their rhythms to America. For these native Africans, rhythm was much more than just a musical element. It was also a language, a spiritual tool, a bedrock of society. African rhythm had a complexity and resonance that was lacking in the European-based music of the American colonists. The slaves also brought with them the call-and-response vocal traditions of their homeland, as well as African percussion and string instruments that resembled the banjo

owerful, emotional, majestic thing called black gospel
layed a part in forming rhythm & blues, and later, as the
nd roll."–Johnny Otis (1994 Hall of Fame Inductee)

and the fiddle. The music of the African slaves had a dynamic, rhythmic charge and an expressive vocal feel that quickly seeped into prevailing American traditions and transformed them. And vice-versa. Slaves learned and modified the Southern folk songs they heard, and much as African-Americans slowly took on the religious rituals of colonial America, so they incorporated certain European-based song forms into their own music. Gospel music–the music of the black church–was, and still is, alive with the resounding rhythms and vocal exhortations of its African heritage. The electric spirit of rock and roll can be traced back to the joyous celebrations of the church. As Little Richard recalls, "You let loose! That piano was talkin', the drums was walkin'. Oh, everybody was gone. You know, people shouting all over the place. And if you didn't understand what it was, you thought you was in a rock and roll concert. That's the way black gospel was when I was a boy." The blues arose around the turn of the century, capturing the sorrows and triumphs of African-American life in the South. By the thirties the blues had developed distinct stylistic strains as personified by two of its greatest artists, vocalist Bessie

Lead Belly

Smith and guitarist, vocalist and composer Robert Johnson, both of whom would die tragic deaths before the decade ended. Smith was an urban star whose magnificent voice was accompanied by pianos and horns on sophisticated recordings that stuck more strictly to a defined blues form. Johnson, on the other hand, was from deep in the Mississippi Delta, where he learned to accompany his achingly emotional voice and haunted lyrics with complex, irregular guitar patterns. Smith's influence can be heard in the early rhythm & blues stars of the forties and fifties just as distinctly as it can be heard in the music of Janis Joplin, who cited Smith as her greatest inspiration. Similarly, Robert Johnson's spirit can be profoundly felt in the electric blues–based style of music from its beginnings in the forties through the blues-rock explosion of the sixties to some of today's hard rock and heavy metal.

The great migration of Southern African-Americans to urban centers in the North in the forties instigated the growth of the tough-minded, electrified form known as Chicago blues. The key artist of that style was Muddy Waters, a Mississippi Delta native who had known Johnson and absorbed the country blues tradition. Up north, bluesmen had begun using amplified instruments in order to be heard in the noisy bars and house parties where they played. By the early fifties Waters was leading the grittiest electric blues band in town, fueled by his authoritative vocals and stinging slide guitar and Little Walter's harmonica. Compare Waters's music of the time with the Rolling Stones' early records, and the stylistic connections

Hank Williams

Bessie Smith

become obvious. Rhythm & blues, the immensely popular music of black America in the forties and early fifties, married the vocal styling and song forms of the blues to the swinging beat of big-band jazz and the rhythmic propulsion of boogie-woogie music. The king of R&B during its late forties heyday was saxophonist, vocalist and band leader Louis Jordan, whose infectious, riotously funny and just plain rocking recordings are direct precursors to rock and roll. Finally, with the inclusion of country music, a new sound began to come together. As white singers and musicians picked up on the blues, African-American players tuned in to country. The country influences heard in the styles of the two fathers of rock and roll—Elvis Presley and Chuck Berry—are proof of this rich, and necessary, cross-pollination.

Between its earliest beginnings and its later forms, rock and roll owes a debt to countless other musicians and styles. The rural folk songs of Lead Belly, the R&B vocalizing of the Orioles, the West Coast "jump" style of Wynonie Harris and Roy Brown, the western swing of Bob Wills, the gritty blues of Elmore James, the country epics of Hank Williams, the guitar styling of T-Bone Walker and B. B. King, the rolling New Orleans sound of Fats Domino; these and a host of other artists and styles all played an integral part in the making of rock and roll. To paraphrase Willie Dixon, the poet laureate and lifelong champion of the blues: Without the roots there are no fruits. When it comes to rock and roll, truer words have never been spoken.

Rhythm & Blues   Rockabilly   British Invasion

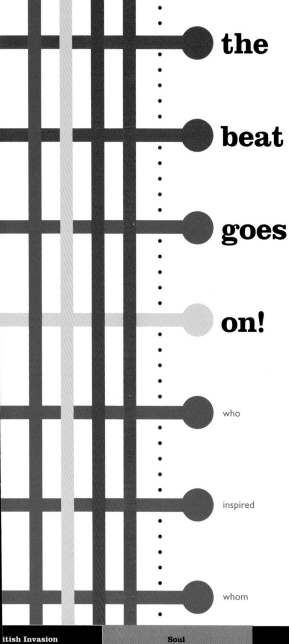

the

beat

goes

on!

who

inspired

whom

No great music, particularly rock and roll, was created in a vacuum. The music of the past exists to be plundered by contemporary artists. Remolded and reshaped, new sounds arise from old. For as it was put by film director Jean-Luc Godard–not quite a rocker, but a genuine rebel nonetheless–it's not what you take, it's where you take it to.

Rhythm & Blues

The great R&B pioneers drew on the music they grew up with in the thirties and forties. Titans of the three major pre–rock and roll musical genres: jazz (Louis Armstrong, Billie Holiday, Fats Waller, Count Basie), blues (Bessie Smith, T-Bone Walker) and gospel (Marion Williams) affected younger artists who went on to devise the new music of the fifties. R&B acts often influenced each other in profound ways. Hank Ballard, the composer of the dance classic "The Twist," admits that the melody for that song was based on an earlier Drifters' tune, "Whatʼcha Gonna Do?" while Little Richard claims that his trademark phrasing of "Lucille-*uh*" was actually taken from Ruth Brown's high-pitched "Mama-*uh*" as heard on her hit "Mama, He Treats Your Daughter Mean."

Rockabilly

The Southern rockabilly artists were heavily influenced by country music. It's no surprise that giants like Hank Williams and the Louvin Brothers are cited here, as are earlier country pioneers, such as Bill Monroe, the father of bluegrass, and Jimmie Rodgers, "The Singing Brakeman," who mixed blues with rural folk music. Artists like Elvis Presley may have been announcing a new era of popular music, but they still had a strong sense of tradition. On his early Sun recordings Presley acknowledged his roots by cutting Monroe's "Blue Moon of Kentucky."

And Monroe appreciated it: "I told him if it helped him get his start and give him the style of music he wanted to do, I was for him one-hundred percent. It was all right."

British Invasion

The mid-sixties British Invasion artists were obsessed with American music of all genres. It's impossible not to hear the impassioned Chicago blues of Muddy Waters in the Rolling Stones, the grit of John Lee Hooker in the tough rock of the Animals, or the softer harmonies of the Everly Brothers in the melodious Hollies. The rough funk of R&B left its mark, too. "The first record I remember was 'Green Onions' by Booker T. and the MGs," said Pete Townshend. "It was their guitarist, Steve Cropper, who really turned me on to aggressive guitar playing." The kids from the U.K. also loved rockabilly; just ask Carl Perkins—the Beatles recorded his "Honey Don't," "Everybody's Trying to Be My Baby," and "Match Box."

Soul

Soul sprung from rhythm & blues and gospel. Little wonder then that such R&B monarchs as James Brown, Clyde McPhatter, Little Willie John and Charles Brown and gospel greats like Clara Ward and Professor Alex Bradford are sprinkled throughout as major influences. "I loved that man's voice to death," said James Brown of his early idol, Little Willie John. "I heard everything I loved in Willie John."

Listen to any of Brown's recordings and Little Willie's spirit can still be heard. Just scratch the surface of a soul record, and its roots pour forth. The key is passion. Soul is nothing if not music from the gut and the heart. Vocalists like Ray Charles and Marvin Gaye sing the truth just as their musical parents taught them how.

Folk Rock

The literate nature of folk rock accounts for the importance of Bob Dylan and the Beatles as its presiding influences. Dylan's emphatic poetry and the Beatles' energy and spirit fostered a wellspring of inspiration for bands as sophisticated as the Byrds as well as more pop-oriented groups like the Turtles. The Byrds' first hit was an electrified reworking of Dylan's "Mr. Tambourine Man," while the Turtles went Top Ten with Dylan's "It Ain't Me Babe." At times, the connections between artists are distant to the listener, but very real to the songwriter. Take the case of the Lovin' Spoonful and their 1965 hit "Daydream." Composer John Sebastian claims that in writing "Daydream," he was directly influenced by the steady rhythms of the Supremes' hit "Baby Love," while also admitting that the two songs sound nothing alike!

Psychedelic

Some say that psychedelic music is just the blues played with the amplifiers on 11. It is undeniable that the blues formed the backbone of so much of the hard-rocking sounds of the mid- to late sixties, accounting for the presence of Robert Johnson, Muddy Waters, Bessie Smith and others as important influences. But in the eclectic spirit of the times, various unexpected source music would creep in. The boozy, debauched revelry of Bertolt Brecht's and Kurt Weill's "Three Penny Opera" must have spoken to the anarchic spirit of the Doors' Jim Morrison. The rousing rendition of Brecht's and Weill's "Alabama Song" from the Doors' debut album could convince you that there was obviously a lot in common between the streetlife of twenties' Berlin and sixties' Los Angeles.

Singer/Songwriters
The naked emotion and soul-searching introspection that characterize the singer/songwriter movement of the sixties and seventies has significant precedents in the work of two rural artists: Hank Williams and Woody Guthrie. In contrast to the middle-class, college-educated backgrounds of the latter-day balladeers, Williams and Guthrie were offspring of the Depression and lived hard-traveling lifestyles. Bob Dylan and Neil Young responded to the integrity and outspoken nature of Williams's and Guthrie's songs. Dylan was hit by the power of Guthrie as a young man in the Midwest: "Either in Minneapolis or St. Paul, I heard Woody Guthrie. And

when I heard Woody Guthrie, that was it, it was all over."

Hard Rock
Sometimes influences seem to come out of left field. It's obvious that Aerosmith did their share of listening to the Rolling Stones and that Metallica love Black Sabbath. But explain the admiration that Axl Rose of Guns n' Roses has for Elton John, or the esteem that Jimmy Page of Led Zeppelin holds for British folk guitarist Bert Jansch. Close listening often reveals that within the heart of a hard rock band lies a reflective, romantic soul. When Rose sings a piano-based ballad, Elton's right alongside him; when Page launches into an acoustic, folk-tinged tune, Jansch's presence is felt. And the same goes for the frivolous side of hard rock. The offhanded asides that became former Van Halen vocalist David Lee Roth's trademark are indebted to Fats Waller, who way back in the thirties was tossing out suggestive lines that would shame Roth.

Punk and New Wave
When a contemporary band acknowledges its influences, it can often result in reviving interest in that band or artist. With the punk and new wave movement of the late seventies and eighties, the names of earlier, overlooked bands began to be bandied about, arousing interest and renewed admiration. The Velvet Underground, the Stooges, the

New York Dolls and Mott the Hoople were, for the most part, rock footnotes. All of a sudden they were being championed by bands such as the Sex Pistols, who looked to the earlier bands as models of unadulterated energy, agression and left-of-center inventiveness. The renewed attention showered on the Velvet Underground transformed them into rock icons; Iggy Pop, leader of the Stooges, has a thriving career, and a Mott the Hoople reunion tour is probably right around the corner.

Alternative
There are times when a band's decisive influence can be one of their contemporaries rather than a figure from the past. Nirvana was already an established band with an album under their belt when they went into the studio to record *Nevermind*. Songwriter Kurt Cobain had been doing some hard listening to a Boston-based band of the time called the Pixies, whose use of dynamics and altered pop-song form particularly impressed him. Cobain used the Pixies as a model in writing "Smells like Teen Spirit," the tune that broke the band into superstardom. "I was basically trying to rip off the Pixies. I have to admit it," Cobain said. "When I heard the Pixies for the first time, I connected with that band so heavily I should have been in that band—or at least in a Pixies cover band."

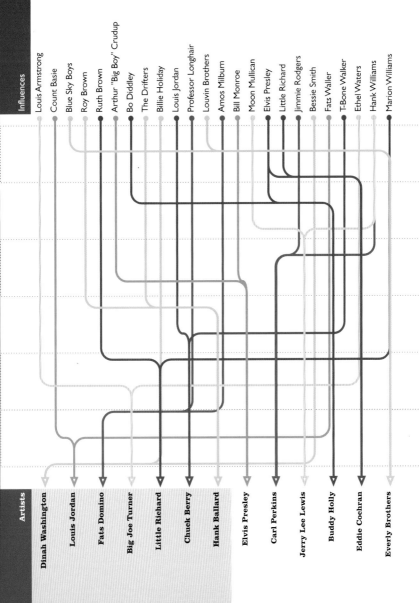

Influences

Louis Armstrong
Count Basie
Blue Sky Boys
Roy Brown
Ruth Brown
Arthur "Big Boy" Crudup
Bo Diddley
The Drifters
Billie Holiday
Louis Jordan
Professor Longhair
Louvin Brothers
Amos Milburn
Bill Monroe
Moon Mullican
Elvis Presley
Little Richard
Jimmie Rodgers
Bessie Smith
Fats Waller
T-Bone Walker
Ethel Waters
Hank Williams
Marion Williams

Artists

Dinah Washington
Louis Jordan
Fats Domino
Big Joe Turner
Little Richard
Chuck Berry
Hank Ballard
Elvis Presley
Carl Perkins
Jerry Lee Lewis
Buddy Holly
Eddie Cochran
Everly Brothers

Rhythm & Blues

Rockabilly

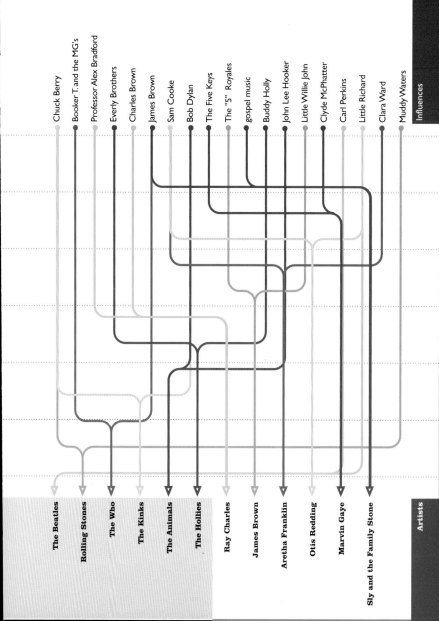

Influences

Chuck Berry
Booker T. and the MG's
Professor Alex Bradford
Everly Brothers
Charles Brown
James Brown
Sam Cooke
Bob Dylan
The Five Keys
The "5" Royales
gospel music
Buddy Holly
John Lee Hooker
Little Willie John
Clyde McPhatter
Carl Perkins
Little Richard
Clara Ward
Muddy Waters

Artists

The Beatles
Rolling Stones
The Who
The Kinks
The Animals
The Hollies
Ray Charles
James Brown
Aretha Franklin
Otis Redding
Marvin Gaye
Sly and the Family Stone

British Invasion

Soul

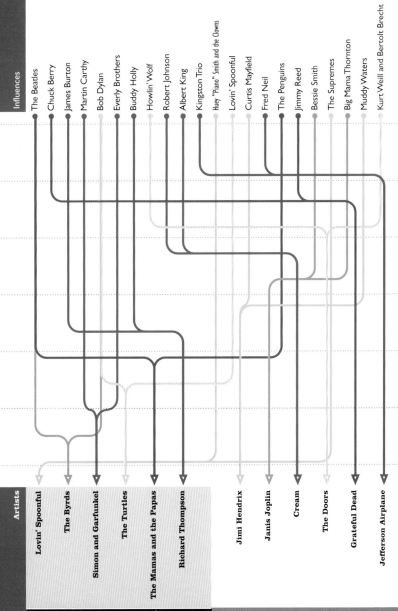

Influences

The Beatles
Chuck Berry
James Burton
Martin Carthy
Bob Dylan
Everly Brothers
Buddy Holly
Howlin' Wolf
Robert Johnson
Albert King
Kingston Trio
Huey "Piano" Smith and the Clowns
Lovin' Spoonful
Curtis Mayfield
Fred Neil
The Penguins
Jimmy Reed
Bessie Smith
The Supremes
Big Mama Thornton
Muddy Waters
Kurt Weill and Bertolt Brecht

Artists

Lovin' Spoonful
The Byrds
Simon and Garfunkel
The Turtles
The Mamas and the Papas
Richard Thompson

Jimi Hendrix
Janis Joplin
Cream
The Doors
Grateful Dead
Jefferson Airplane

Folk Rock

Psychedelic

Influences

Aerosmith
Chuck Berry
Black Sabbath
Ray Charles
Eric Clapton
Judy Collins
Alice Cooper
Elizabeth Cotton
Diamond Head
Willie Dixon
Bob Dylan
Woody Guthrie
Bert Jansch
Elton John
Led Zeppelin
Roy Orbison
Rolling Stones
Fats Waller
Hank Williams
Stevie Wonder
Yardbirds

Artists

Bruce Springsteen
Bob Dylan
Neil Young
Joni Mitchell
James Taylor
Led Zeppelin
Kiss
Metallica
Aerosmith
Guns n' Roses
Van Halen

Singer/Songwriter

Hard Rock

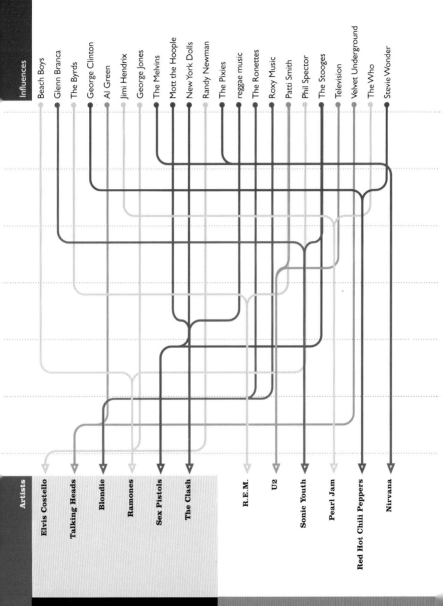

Influences

Beach Boys
Glenn Branca
The Byrds
George Clinton
Al Green
Jimi Hendrix
George Jones
The Melvins
Mott the Hoople
New York Dolls
Randy Newman
The Pixies
reggae music
The Ronettes
Roxy Music
Patti Smith
Phil Spector
The Stooges
Television
Velvet Underground
The Who
Stevie Wonder

Artists

Elvis Costello
Talking Heads
Blondie
Ramones
Sex Pistols
The Clash
R.E.M.
U2
Sonic Youth
Pearl Jam
Red Hot Chili Peppers
Nirvana

Punk and New Wave

Alternative

1

Rock and Roll Archaeology: Ten Treasures

1970

Boots: Belonged to Patti Smith, singer/poet
Description: c. 1970, combat-style, black boots,
8 in. tall x 3 1/2 in. x 10 1/2 in.
Worn during the tours of the late seventies
Rock and Roll Hall of Fame and Museum.
Gift of Beverly Smith

Patti Smith has one of the most impressive extra-musical resumes in rock history. A published poetess and former rock critic, Smith also collaborated on a play with Sam Shepard. She knew the right collaborators to work with once she became a star as well: her biggest hit, 1978's "Because the Night," was a joint effort with Bruce Springsteen.

1959

Report card: Belonged to Keith Moon, drummer for the Who

Description: Issued by Alperton Secondary School for Boys, 1959. C average with A minus in music

Rock and Roll Hall of Fame and Museum. Gift of Kit Moon

Although he was showing promise in music, school may not have been the highest priority for Keith Moon. By the time he was seventeen, Moon was a working member of the Who, pounding—and regularly destroying—his drums with manic intensity. Rock's premier madman, Moon once drove a car into a hotel swimming pool during a 1967 tour the Who shared with Herman's Hermits.

MIDDLESEX EDUCATION COMMITTEE

ALPERTON SECONDARY SCHOOL FOR BOYS

REPORT FOR *Summer* TERM, 1959

Name of Pupil *Keith Moon* Form *2ᵃ*

ASSESSMENTS: A—Excellent; B—Good; C—Fair; D—Weak; E—Very Weak

SUBJECT	MARKS: EXAM. TERM	COMMENT	INITIALS
ENGLISH	42% B–	Began to work more seriously some time ago. The effect continues. "Good!"	
ENGLISH LITERATURE			
FRENCH	62% C+	He can do good work, but is off, & late.	C.H.
GEOGRAPHY	40% C+	Lively & original but sometimes slack & careless	
HISTORY	11% C+	Not enough subject matter below the bright surface	
MATHEMATICS	11/2 C+	Talent and temperament mixed, & 2 but the two seem well stressed little has been retained	
SCIENCE	56% C	Superficially interested — lacks concentration	
TECHNICAL DRAWING			
METALWORK	C	Fails it on effort physically but is low. H.	
WOODWORK	C–		
ART	3/10 D	Impatient, although does better work	
MUSIC	77% A–	particular ease with courage and tactics and in exam. He shows considerable ability	C.H.
PHYSICAL EDUCATION	C+	Works well at times, but is still inclined to play the fool.	

Attendance 319/400

General Remarks: *Behaviour good. He is more sensible in his manner. His personality assures him of some standing with the rest of the boys in the form. Academically he is in the lower half.*

Form Master *R.Wilkinson* Headmaster

NEXT TERM BEGINS *Tuesday 8ᵗʰ September*

Mr & Mrs Moon
134, Chaplin Road
Wembley
Middx

1970s

Stage outfit Belonged to Bootsy Collins, bassist for Parliament-Funkadelic
Description: fully-fringed shirt and pants
Rock and Roll Hall of Fame and Museum,
Gift of Bootsy Collins

Bassist and vocalist Bootsy Collins came to the P-Funk universe from a stint with the greatest R&B finishing school there was: James Brown's band. With George Clinton's P-Funk conglomerations and his own Bootsy's Rubber Band, Collins became a hero to a new generation of musicians. Collins is even celebrated by name in the Tom Tom Club's 1982 hit, "Genius of Love."

Flamboyant costumes and elaborate props combined with attitude to distinguish P-Funk's "one nation under a groove."

1950s

Saxophone: Belonged to Louis Jordan, R&B saxo-
phonist, vocalist and band leader
Description: 25³/₈ in. × 8¹/₂ in. × 4³/₄ in. deep
Rock and Roll Hall of Fame and Museum.
Gift of Martha Jordan

Louis Jordan, one of the fathers of rock and roll,
had deep roots in the swing era of the thirties.
Jordan first attracted attention in drummer Chick
Webb's big band, playing alto saxophone and
singing, alongside famed vocalist Ella Fitzgerald.
Jordan was a major influence on three of the
most important figures in the formation of rock
and roll: Chuck Berry, Ray Charles and B. B. King.
Jordan's influence continues to be felt today. His
vintage hits, with their jumping beat and clever
lyrics, were the inspiration for the Broadway
musical *Five Guys Named Moe.*

1948

Guitar: Belonged to Elmore James, blues guitarist extraordinaire.
Description: c. 1948 National, 42 in. x 15 1/2 in. x 4 1/2 in.
Rock and Roll Hall of Fame and Museum.
Gift of Bobby Robinson

Elmore James's songs helped form a repertoire for the sixties blues-rock movement, among them: "Dust My Broom," "The Sky Is Crying," "Done Somebody Wrong," "I Can't Hold Out" and "It Hurts Me Too."

James's stinging guitar work and anguished vocals influenced such major rock figures as Jimi Hendrix, Eric Clapton, Duane Allman and Jeff Beck.

1968

Jacket: Belonged to Jimi Hendrix, psychedelic/blues guitarist
Description: velvet patchwork, 20 in. across shoulders, 23 1/2 in. long
Rock and Roll Hall of Fame and Museum.
Gift of James Alan Hendrix

Jimi Hendrix's unique sartorial style pulled together a variety of influences reflecting the guitarist's personal background and professional experiences.

Hendrix's flamboyant garb mixed the funky flash of the R&B players with whom he worked in the early sixties, the psychedelic Carnaby Street fashions, which coincided with his commerical breakthrough in the mid-sixties, and Native American attire, an acknowledgment of Hendrix's mixed ethnic roots.

1966

Lyric sheet: "Purple Haze," 1966
Written by Jimi Hendrix for the album *Are You Experienced?* 1967
Originally titled "Purple Haze, Jesus Saves."
Description: 8 in. x 5 in. Written by Hendrix in the dressing room of the Upper Cut Club in London. This is the first known draft of the song. These lyrics were thrown away by Hendrix and retrieved from the trash by a friend.
Rock and Roll Hall of Fame and Museum. Gift of the Rock and Roll Hall of Fame Foundation

Jimi Hendrix had to leave America to make it big in America. Discovered by Animals' bassist Chas Chandler, Hendrix was brought to England in 1966 to groom his act. With the addition of drummer Mitch Mitchell and bassist Noel Redding, the Jimi Hendrix Experience was formed; hits in the U.K., like "Hey Joe," soon followed. Hendrix's first U.S. appearance after the formation of his band was his celebrated performance at the Monterey Pop Festival in June 1967. In that same summer, Hendrix captivated America with his "Purple Haze" single and its "scuse me while I kiss the sky" refrain.

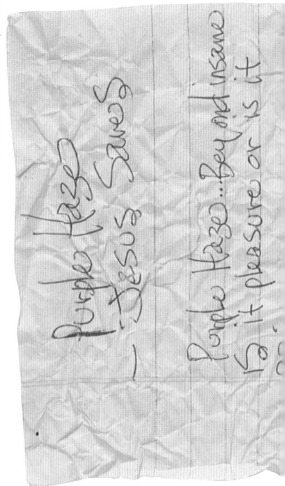

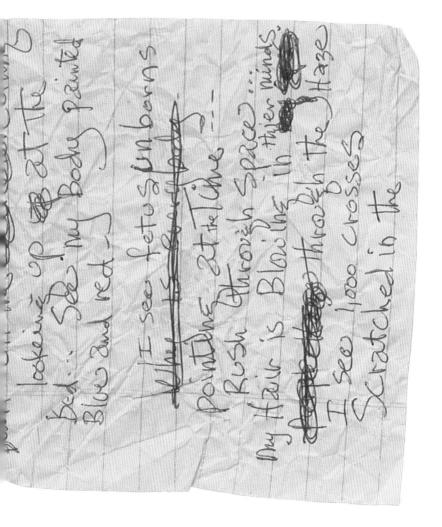

looking up at the
bed... See my Body painted
Blue and red

I see fetus Unborns

Pointing at the Time ---
Rush through space ...
My Hair is Blowing in thier minds
through the Haze
I see 1,000 crosses
Scratched in the

1959

Jacket; Belonged to Carl Gardner of the Coasters
Description: black tuxedo jacket with gold sequins, 18½ in. across shoulders, 18¾ in. across chest, 27 in. arm length, 33¾ in. long
Rock and Roll Hall of Fame and Museum. Gift of Carl Gardner

The Coasters were a California-based vocal group who originally started out as the Robins. The clown princes of rock and roll will always be associated with Jerry Leiber and Mike Stoller, the writing and producing team that gave them such amusing, unforgettable fifties hits as "Yakety Yak," "Charlie Brown" and "Poison Ivy," titles that are emblazoned on Gardner's jacket.

1975

Guitar: Belonged to David Byrne of Talking Heads
Description: 1975 12-string Angelica
42³/₄ in. x 16 in. x 4³/₈ in.—2 in. width at top of neck
Rock and Roll Hall of Fame and Museum.
Gift of Tina Weymouth and Chris Frantz

Talking Heads had its genesis at the Rhode Island School of Design, where David Byrne, Tina Weymouth and Chris Franz first met. Before hooking up with Jerry Harrison, the Talking Heads originally played as a trio. Keyboardist/guitarist Harrison already had his proto-New Wave credentials in order: he had been a member of the legendary band Jonathan Richman and the Modern Lovers.

Much of the group's early popular appeal was linked to its fun-loving, quirky, sometimes neurotic lyrics and to its exacting instrumentals, including Byrne's simple, refined guitar phrasing.

1948

Sheet music and 78 rpm record: "It's Too Soon to Know," 1948, written by Deborah Chessler for the Orioles

Description: Commercial sheet music, 12 in. x 9 in., and Natural 78 rpm record. Rock and Roll Hall of Fame and Museum. Gift of Deborah Chessler in memory of her mother

"It's Too Soon To Know" is considered by many noted pop-music historians to be the first rock and roll song. It was composed by a young Deborah Chessler, who went on to manage the Orioles, one of the most important of the early R&B vocal bands.

IT'S TOO SOON TO KNOW

By Deborah Chessler

An Originally Introduced And Recorded by
The Orioles
on NATURAL RECORD No. 5000

EDWIN H. MORRIS & COMPANY
music publishers

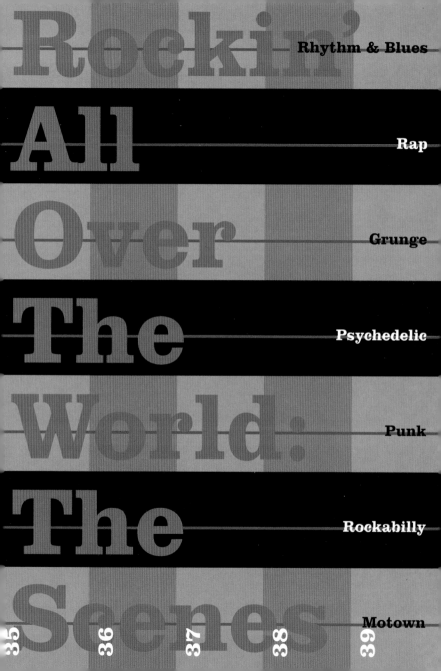

Rockin' All Over The World: The Scenes

Rhythm & Blues

Rap

Grunge

Psychedelic

Punk

Rockabilly

Motown

35   36   37   38   39

New Orle

Rhythm & Blues

New York

Rap

Seattle

Grunge

San Fran

Psychedelic

London/N

Punk

Memphis

Rockabilly

Detroit

Motown

40   41   42   43   44

1945
January: Cosimo Matassa opens J&M Studio. All the best New Orleans rhythm & blues records of the next 25 years, including Fats Domino's, are made under his tutelage.

1948
June: Roy Brown debuts on the charts with the rhythm & blues classic "Good Rockin' Tonight."

Rap

1949
December: Fats Domino cuts "The Fat Man," with Dave Bartholomew producing.

Professor Longhair is recorded for the first time. His four-song session yields the anthem "Mardi Gras in New Orleans."

isco

1948
October: Memphis station WDIA changes to an all-black format. By the following summer, it will become the first radio station in the U.S. staffed entirely by black disc jockeys, and in a few years, it will be the most powerful station in Memphis.

sychedelic

YC

Winter: "Daddy-O-Dewey" Phillips takes over the "Red Hot and Blue" show on WHBQ, programming a mix of hillbilly, blues and pop music.

1949
July: Nashville's Bullet Records releases the first record by Memphis-based Riley "B. B." King, host of a popular show on WDIA.

Rockabilly

Motown

45 46 47 48 49

New Orle

Rhythm & Blues

Rap

G...

P...ic

Punk

Ro...abilly

Motown

New Yo...k

Seattle

...o Fra...

Londo... A...

Memphis

Detro...

1952
May: "Lawdy Miss Clawdy," a huge New Orleans–flavored R&B hit by Lloyd Price, with Domino guesting on piano, hits Number One.

1954
February: Guitar Slim's seminal R&B song, "The Things That I Used To Do," becomes a national hit.

1950
January: Sam C. Phillips opens Memphis Recording Service at 706 Union Avenue, the site of a former radiator repair shop. He begins recording several local blues artists, including B. B. King, Howlin' Wolf and James Cotton.

1951
March: Phillips records "Rocket 88" with singer Jackie Brenston and Ike Turner's band. The record is released by the Chess label and is an R&B smash.

1954
July: Sun releases "That's All Right" and "Blue Moon of Kentucky" by Elvis Presley, backed by guitarist Scotty Moore and bassist Bill Black. Dewey Phillips debuts the record on "Red, Hot and Blue."

1955
November: Despite Presley's growing popularity, his five Sun singles fail to make a dent on the national charts. Phillips sells his contract to RCA Records for $35,000.

December: Carl Perkins records "Blue Suede Shoes" and "Honey Don't," which Sun releases together as a single on January 1, 1956. It will become Sun's first million-seller.

1952
March: Phillips launches his own label, Sun Records.

1953
March: WDIA disc jockey Rufus Thomas' "Bear Cat," an answer record to Big Mama Thornton's "Hound Dog," becomes Sun's first national hit.

50　51　52　53　54

1959 February: Frankie Ford records "Sea Cruise," backed by famed New Orleans pianist Huey Smith, for the Louisiana-based Ace Records.

1955 September: Little Richard travels to New Orleans, where he records "Tutti Frutti" at the end of the session.

1956 October: Shirley and Lee's "Let the Good Times Roll," a million-seller, peaks at Number 20 on the charts.

1959 "Come to Me," by Marv Johnson, is the debut release on the Tamla label. Founded by Berry Gordy, Tamla is the first of several labels under the umbrella of his Motown Records Corporation.

1959 December: Hi Records scores its first big hit, "Smokie, Part 2," by the Bill Black Combo. In the next decade, the label will become influential in the development of soul music, with a roster of artists including Al Green.

1957 August: Huey "Piano" Smith and the Clowns' single "Rockin' Pneumonia and the Boogie Woogie Flu," a syncopated rock and roll classic, debuts on the charts.

1957 March: Sun releases "Whole Lotta Shakin' Goin' On," by Jerry Lee Lewis.

Grunge

"Bad Girl," by the Miracles, is the first single released on the Motown label. The name is a contraction of "Motor Town," a reference to Detroit's status as the center of the auto industry.

November: "Great Balls of Fire" hits Number One. Near the end of the year, Jerry Lee Lewis marries his 13-year-old cousin, Myra Gale Brown.

Psychedelic

Berry Gordy moves all of Motown's recording and administrative operations into a two-story house at 2648 West Grand Boulevard, which he christens "Hitsville."

Winter: Inspired by the success of Sun, Quinton Claunch, Bill Cantrell and Ray Harris form Hi Records. Joe Cuoghi, owner of Memphis' Poplar Tunes record store, becomes the label's president.

Punk

Rockabilly

May: Sun releases Johnny Cash's "I Walk the Line," which hits Number Two on the country chart and Number 19 on the pop chart.

1956 April: Roy Orbison's first Sun single, "Ooby Dooby," is released.

where he is blacklisted from radio playlists and numerous bookings are canceled.

1958 May: While on tour in England, Jerry Lee Lewis is attacked by the press, who are outraged by his marriage. The furor carries back to the U.S.,

New Orle

Rhythm & Blues

Rap

Grunge

Psychedelic

Punk

Rockabilly

Motown

1961
May: Vocalist Ernie K-Doe's "Mother-in-Law," a million-selling novelty, hits Number One. The song was released by Minit Records, one of the most important independent labels in New Orleans.

1961
January: Motown signs the Primettes, a girl group just out of high school. They change their name to the Supremes.

February: "Shop Around," by the Miracles, is Motown's first national hit, reaching Number Two on the Billboard chart and topping Billboard's Hot R&B singles list for eight weeks.

December: "Please Mr. Postman," by the Marvelettes, becomes Motown's first Number One pop hit and second million-seller.

ns

Rhythm & Blues

Rap

Grunge

Psychedelic

Punk

Rockabilly

Motown

1964
New Orleans singer Tina Thomas cuts "Time Is On My Side," an R&B hit subsequently covered by the Rolling Stones.

1963
August: Motown's 12-year-old prodigy, Little Stevie Wonder, tops the pop charts with "Fingertips (Pt. II)." Recorded in concert, it is the first live single in history to reach Number One.

1964
August: Martha and the Vandellas release "Dancing in the Street," one of the definitive anthems in rock and roll history and a highlight of Motown's early years.

1962
March: The Temptations, another vocal group signed to Motown, release their first single "Dream Come True" on the Gordy label.

63

64

New Orle

New York

Seattle

San Fran

Detroit

1965
R May: The Dixie Cups, a female vocal trio, top the national singles chart with "Chapel of Love." A year later they score another hit with "Iko Iko," based on a Creole chant.

1965
June: "Back in My Arms Again" tops the Billboard Hot 100 singles chart, making the Supremes the only American group to release five Number One hits in a row.

Psyche

1965
June: The Red Dog Saloon opens for business in Virginia City, Nevada, and the San Francisco–based Charlatans are the house band.

August: The Matrix, a pizza parlor turned rock club, is opened by Marty Balin of Jefferson Airplane. The still-legal hallucinogen LSD is sold at the bar.

Motown

1966
July: Soul singer Lee Dorsey scores the biggest record of his career when "Working In A Coal Mine," written by Allen Toussaint, hits Number Eight in both America and the U.K.

December: "Tell It Like It Is," featuring the vocals of Aaron Neville, rises to Number Two on the national charts.

December: Ken Kesey and his Merry Pranksters throw the first Acid Test—a chaotic party spiked with psychedelic drugs—in San Jose. The Grateful Dead, then known as the Warlocks, provide the music.

1966
October: The Four Tops earn their second Number One single and the biggest hit of their career with "Reach Out, I'll Be There." It is one of many written and produced for them by the team of Brian Holland, Lamont Dozier, and Eddie Holland.

October: A Tribute to Dr. Strange, an evening of music, dance and light shows, is organized by pioneering promoters the Family Dog. Performing at the event are Jefferson Airplane, the Charlatans, and the Great Society.

November: Bill Graham presents his first show, a benefit for the San Francisco Mime Troupe.

1966
January: The Psychedelic Shop opens in Haight-Ashbury, selling books, records, roach clips and other accoutrements of the hippie lifestyle.

Ken Kesey plans, and Bill Graham supervises, the Trips Festival: three days of concerts, films, readings and lights.

1967
December: "I Heard It Through the Grapevine," written by Marvin Gaye and recorded by Gladys Knight and the Pips, rises to Number Two. Exactly a year later, Gaye's own version will become the top song in the country.

February: Big Brother and Holding Company and Jefferson Airplane headline the Tribal Stomp

October: A new federal law makes possession of LSD illegal.

65

66

67

1968
Summer: A young singing group, the Jackson Five, auditions for Berry Gordy at the Motown offices. Fronted by nine-year-old Michael Jackson, they are signed on the spot.

December: Motown records occupy the three top spots on Billboard's Hot 100, an unprecedented feat.

1969
December: A free concert organized by the Rolling Stones turns ugly at Altamont Speedway, outside San Francisco. Sets are disrupted by violence from Hell's Angels. Marty Balin is knocked unconscious and a concertgoer is stabbed to death.

1967
January: The Human Be-In, subtitled A Gathering of the Tribes, is held in Golden Gate Park, drawing an estimated 20,000.

"Hello Hello" by Sopwith Camel becomes the first single by a San Francisco band to break the Top Forty.

April: The Gray Line tour company announces the Hippie Hop, a bus trip through Haight-Ashbury for curious tourists.

June: The Monterey Pop Festival provides worldwide exposure for the San Francisco bands.

August: Beatle George Harrison and his wife, Patti, stroll the streets of Haight-Ashbury, bringing more international attention to the scene.

1968
July: Bill Graham takes over the Carousel, a club jointly owned by Jefferson Airplane and the Grateful Dead, and rechristens it Fillmore West.

1969
February: The Temptations win Motown its first Grammy for "Cloud Nine." It is the first in a series of topical, street-savvy singles that signal a new direction for Motown and the band.

n & Blues

Rap

Grunge

Psychedelic

Punk

nabilly

Motown

68

69

New Ou[t]

1970
Rhythm & **Blues**

May: Diana Ross leaves the Supremes to go solo.

July: Edwin Starr's "War," composed by Motown songwriter and producer **Ra**Norman Whitfield, becomes a major hit and provocative anti-war anthem.

October: With the success of **Gr**"I'll Be There," the Jackson Five become the only group in history whose first four records went to Number One. "I'll Be There" is also the biggest-selling Motown single to date

Psychedelic

Punk

1971
May: Marvin Gaye releases What's Going On, a thematic, self-produced masterwork whose songs tackle such subjects as **Rockabilly** Vietnam, social conditions, and the environment.

1975
November: Patti Smith's landmark debut album, Horses, is released. Beat poetry and garage rock meet in this early blueprint for punk rock and new wave.

1975
Jamaican Kool DJ Herc hosts parties and shows at Havalo, a club in the Bronx, talking to the crowd while repeatedly playing rythmic, instrumental sections of records (called "breaks").

1976
January: The first issue of Punk magazine is published in New York. Lou Reed is on the cover; the Ramones are featured inside.

1976
April: The first Ramones album, entitled Ramones, is released. Recorded for only $6,000, it contains fourteen songs, none over two minutes.

July: The Ramones perform at the Roundhouse in London. They are approached by future members of the Clash, the Pretenders, the Damned and the Sex Pistols and asked how to form a band.

July: Sniffin' Glue, the first British punk fanzine, hits the streets. It is photocopied, featuring hand-drawn graphics and articles written "For Punks."

August: Stiff Records, the most significant independent label of the era, releases its first single: "So It Goes/Heart of the City," by Nick Lowe.

New York
Seattle
San Fran
London/N
Memphis
Detroit

70 71 72 73 74

1977
January: Patti Smith falls offstage while performing in Tampa, Florida, breaking her neck. During her recuperation, she writes a book of poetry and readies her breakthrough third album, Easter.

March: The Clash sign with CBS for £100,000 advance and record their milestone first album, The Clash, in two weekends.

November: Never Mind the Bollocks, Here's the Sex Pistols is released in the U.S. Ten years later, it is certified gold (500,000 copies sold).

October: Seattle Rocket, a monthly paper documenting the music scene, begins publication.

1979 Subterranean Pop, a xeroxed fanzine devoted to underground American music, publishes its first issue.

1979
Three seminal rap singles are released: "King Time III (Personality Jock)" by the Fatback Band, "Rapper's Delight" by the Sugarhill Gang, and "Christmas Rappin'" by Kurtis Blow.

Rap

1977
February: Talking Heads' first single, "Love Goes to Building On Fire/New Feeling," is released on Sire Records. The group's debut album, Talking Heads '77, is issued in July.

1978
The Bronx club Disco Fever becomes known as "hip-hop's first home."

1979
February: Sid Vicious, the Sex Pistols' bassist, is found dead of a heroin overdose in a Manhattan apartment. At the time he was facing a second-degree murder charge for the fatal knifing of his girlfriend, Nancy Spungen.

1979
April: "Heart of Glass," by Blondie, becomes the first new wave hit to reach Number One in America. The group tops the singles chart three more times in the next two years.

...edelic

G...e

YC

1978
January: The Sex Pistols perform a tumultuous final concert at San Francisco's Winterland Ballroom. They break up soon after.

Rockabilly

December: The Sex Pistols shock a nation when they are goaded into cursing on a TV talk show. Headlines: "The Filth and the Fury," "The Foul Mouthed Yobs," "The Punks—Rotten and Proud of It!" The group is dropped by EMI.

November: "(I Belong to the) Blank Generation," by Richard Hell and the Voidoids, is released on Ork Records. "Blank Generation" defines the punks much as "Beat Generation" described an earlier movement of dropouts and literati.

1976
October: The Sex Pistols sign to EMI Records, receiving a £40,000 advance. They record their first single, "Anarchy in the U.K.," two days later.

Motown

'75   '76   '77   '78   '79

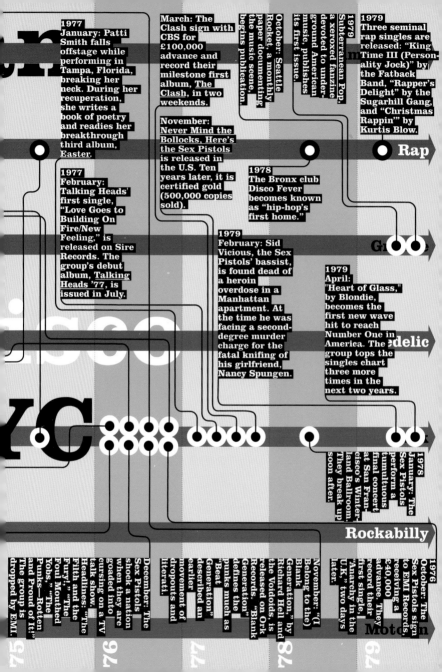

Rhythm & Blues

Rap

New Orle...
New York
Seattle
Gr...
San...
London/N...
Memphis
Detroit

1983
March: Run-D.M.C. emerge as pioneers of rap's "new school" with the release of "It's Like That/Sucker MCs," hailed as the first b-boy (bad boy) single in rap.

1980
January: <u>London Calling</u>, by the Clash, is released. Critics hail it as the best album of the eighties.

1982
April: Afrika Bambaataa and Soulsonic Force release "Planet Rock," which draws heavily on the electronic music of such an unlikely source as Kraftwerk.

1984
December: Run-D.M.C. become the first rappers to earn a gold album for their self-titled debut. They go on to earn rap's first platinum album (1985's <u>The King of Rock</u>) and first multiplatinum album (1986's Raising Hell).

Psychedelic

1981
March: "Rapture," a single by Blondie that acknowledges rap and mentions Grandmaster Flash and Fab 5 Freddy by name, hits Number One.

July: "The Message," a landmark rap about life on the streets, by Grandmaster Flash and the Furious Five, is released.

1985
October: The first rap movie, <u>Krush Groove</u>, is released. It stars the Fat Boys, Kurtis Blow and others.

P...k

April: "The Adventures of Grandmaster Flash on the Wheels of Steel," by Grandmaster Flash and the Furious Five, introduces the techniques of "break-mixing" and "sampling" on vinyl.

Rockabilly

Motown

80 81 82 83 84

Rhythm ...

Rap

Psychedelic

Punk

Motown

1987
March: License to III by the Beastie Boys, a trio of white punk-rockers-turned-rappers from Queens, becomes the first hip-hop album to hit Number One on the pop chart.

August: Boogie Down Productions, featuring rapper KRS-One, releases Criminal Minded, an album that serves as the blueprint for the often violent and sexist gangsta rap.

1989
October: Queen Latifah emerges as rap's foremost female icon with the release of her debut album, All Hail the Queen.

1985
May: One of the first records released by an underground Seattle band, Green River's Come On Down, appears on Homestead Records.

1988
January: Nirvana cut a ten-song demo tape with producer/recordist Jack Endino, Seattle's "Godfather of Grunge," at Reciprocal Recording.

1986
July: Sub Pop 100, a vinyl sampler of the noise-band scene, is released. It includes songs by such Northwest bands as the Wipers and U-Men, as well as influential acts from outside the area like Big Black and Sonic Youth.

1987
June: Green River release their Dry As A Bone EP on the Sub Pop label. This seminal Seattle band includes future members of Pearl Jam and Mudhoney.

The Melvins, a trio whose anti-commercial daring heavily influenced Nirvana, release Gluey Porch Treatments. It captures the darker, sludgier side of the Seattle scene.

October: Soundgarden debuts with Screaming Life, an early example of the grunge sound, released on Sub Pop.

1988
August: Mudhoney release "Touch Me, I'm Sick," the all-time classic grunge single.

November: Nirvana's first single, "Love Buzz/Big Cheese," appears on Sub Pop.

December: Sub Pop 200, a three-EP boxed set, documents the Seattle music scene at an early creative peak. Bands represented on the compilation include Soundgarden, Mudhoney, Beat Happening, Screaming Trees, and Nirvana.

1989
March: Andrew Wood, singer of Mother Love Bone, dies of a drug overdose. A group of Seattle musicians, recording as Temple of the Dog, later cuts an album in tribute to Wood.

June: Bleach, the first Nirvana album, is released. The ten-song LP cost $606.17 to make and was recorded in three nights.

1986
September: Rock meets rap in "Walk This Way," a collaboration between Run-D.M.C. and Aerosmith.

December: Salt-N-Pepa, one of the first female rap groups, makes their debut with the album Hot, Cool & Vicious.

85   86   87   88   89

Rhythm & Blues

Rap

Grunge

Psychedelic

Punk

Rockabilly

Motown

1991
April: <u>Facelift</u>, the debut album by Alice in Chains, enters the charts. The four-member Seattle band embodies grunge's stylistic cross between heavy metal and punk rock.

September: Nirvana release <u>Nevermind</u>, their major-label debut, and Pearl Jam issues <u>Ten</u>, their first album. Both eventually top the charts, establishing the Seattle sound as a major movement in rock and roll.

1992
October: The "grunge look" is co-opted by the fashion industry. Models take to the runway in grunge attire, turning what had been dressing down out of necessity into a dubious fashion statement.

December: Nirvana's <u>Nevermind</u> hits Number One on <u>Billboard</u>'s Top 200 Albums chart. It grosses $50 million in sales.

1994
April: Kurt Cobain, of Nirvana, commits suicide. <u>Live Through This</u>, the second album by Hole—fronted by Courtney Love, Cobain's wife—is released four days earlier.

December: Owners of Sub Pop sell a 49 percent share of the company to Warner Music Group for $20 million.

90 91 92 93 94

In the end, rock and roll comes down to the song. Image and style are important, but the legendary rock and rollers are remembered for their songs: Chuck Berry and "Johnny B. Goode," John Lennon and "Imagine," Bob Dylan and "Like a Rolling Stone," Bruce Springsteen and "Born to Run." A great performance of a great song is what makes the music magical. But what is a great rock and roll song and where does one come from? Do the lyrics come first, or the music? What happens in the recording studio? There are no set answers to those questions. Pete Townshend says that a song comes from "an *inner* thing…. It doesn't come from space," but Keith Richards maintains that "with songwriting, you're more of a receiver … a medium…. I think songs are all around us." Some artists, like Jackson Browne and Paul Simon, work diligently at their craft, drafting and re-drafting songs until they get them right, while others are able to knock out a classic in a matter of minutes. The same is true in the studio. Back in the mid-sixties, when the Kinks recorded "Dedicated Follower of Fashion" and Aretha Franklin recorded "I Never Loved a Man," a song was cut in a few hours, at most. These days, artists can spend months in a studio, laying down numerous versions of a song, and overdubbing instruments and vocals, until the final version sounds almost nothing like the original. Every artist has his or her own way of working, and every song has its own story. There is no single formula. The stories that reveal the unique creative process of making a song are as varied as the artists themselves.…

Jackson Browne began writing songs while still a teenager; one of his best-known, "These Days," was composed when he was 16. By the time Browne released his first album in 1972, his songs had been recorded and performed by Nitty Gritty Dirt Band, Nico, Tom Rush, the Byrds, Bonnie Raitt, Linda Ronstadt and others. During the seventies, Browne established himself as a preeminent West Coast singer-songwriter, composing and performing deeply felt, intensely personal songs like "Late for the Sky," "For a Dancer," and "The Pretender." In the eighties, he broadened his scope and became one of rock's most outspoken political voices. "Sky Blue and Black" was written for Browne's 1993 album, *I'm Alive*. The song started with the title, which, Browne said, "means a sky is sometimes black and sometimes brilliant blue. . . . It also represents the extremes of a relationship." Like many of his songs, "Sky Blue and Black" had a long gestation period. "The first verse came to me probably a year or two before I was willing to go on," he said. Browne went into the studio to record the song before it was complete, and various parts of the final version were shaped by his backup singers and musicians. The music initially had been based on an idea he and longtime collaborator David Lindley had explored onstage literally years before; during the writing, the influence of Lindley's violin gave way to a guitar part Scott Thurston was playing. In the end, Browne said, "The writing of a song is a search. It reflects a question in your life, and hopefully you have answered it by the time you have finished the song."

Jackson Browne

The Kinks

Pete Townshend of the Who has said that Ray Davies "should be made poet laureate of England." As lead singer and songwriter for the Kinks, Davies is responsible for numerous rock classics, ranging from raucous early hits like "You Really Got Me" and "All Day and All of the Night," which laid the groundwork for power-chord-driven hard rock, to gorgeous ballads, like "Waterloo Sunset," which one critic has proclaimed "the most beautiful song in the English language." Davies wrote "Dedicated Follower of Fashion" in 1966, when his songwriting was undergoing a transition. Having decided to "stop writing for other people and start writing for myself," he brought a more personal point of view to his material. In the case of "Dedicated Follower," that manifested itself in the form of satire. Written after a dinner party, the song was intended as a put-down of the then-fashionable Carnaby Street–Swinging London scene. Oddly, it was misinterpreted and has come to be seen as something of a fashion anthem. The song was recorded quickly, and Davies attributes some of its unique sound to happenstance: the rusty strings on his acoustic guitar gave it a tinny tone; his brother, Dave, insisted on playing his new electric guitar; producer Shel Talmy had hired noted pianist Nicky Hopkins for the session, so Ray devised a part for him on the spot. The song was a Top Ten hit in England. In the U.S., it reached Number 36. Davies and the Kinks went on to record a series of concept albums in the late sixties and early seventies and have recorded numerous other hits, including "Victoria," "Lola," "Sleepwalker" and "Come Dancing."

Aretha Franklin was only 24 when she signed with Atlantic Records in November 1966, but she had already been making records for much of her life, first as a child gospel singer, then as a pop singer of only modest success. Though Franklin lacked a strong sense of artistic direction, Atlantic's Jerry Wexler had a strategy: "My attitude was simply to get some great songs, some great players, put Aretha back on piano and let the lady wail." To accomplish his goal, Wexler took Franklin to Rick Hall's Fame Studios in Muscle Shoals, Alabama, where Atlantic had recorded numerous soul hits using such session greats as guitarist Jimmy Johnson, keyboardist Spooner Oldham and drummer Roger Hawkins. The session, with Franklin playing piano and singing, took place on January 24, 1967. The first song recorded that day was "I Never Loved a Man (The Way I Love You)." It took only a few hours. Franklin and the house band then went to work on "Do Right Woman." The song had been written by Chips Moman and Dan Penn, two Memphis-based musicians who had been invited to attend the session. By the end of the day, however, only the rhythm track had been successfully recorded—and by the next day, after a night of fighting between Hall and Aretha's husband-manager, Ted White, Franklin had left Muscle Shoals. Wexler wound up finishing the track with Franklin at Atlantic Studios in New York, adding her vocal and piano parts, as well as background vocals. The resulting record was a two-sided smash and set the stage for Franklin to become the Queen of Soul.

Aretha Franklin

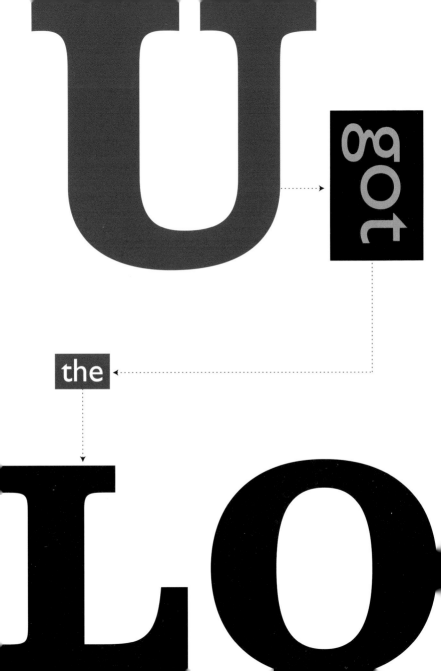

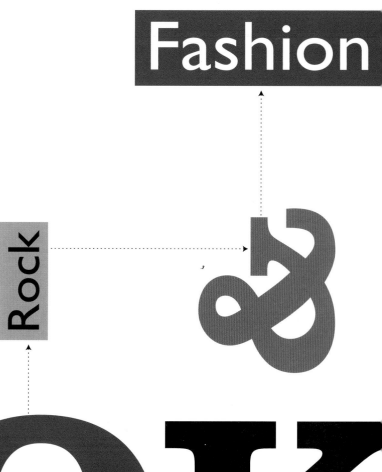

Fashion

Rock

OK

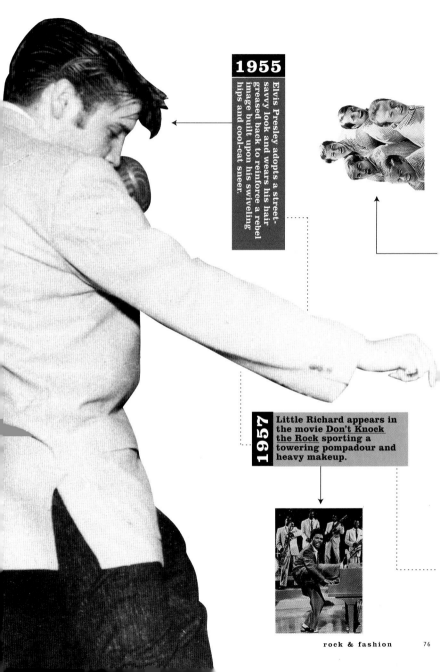

1955

Elvis Presley adopts a street-savvy look and wears his hair greased back to reinforce a rebel image built upon his swiveling hips and cool-cat sneer.

1957

Little Richard appears in the movie <u>Don't Knock the Rock</u> sporting a towering pompadour and heavy makeup.

1963

The clean-cut West Coast surfer look—Pendleton shirts, khaki pants, and close-cropped peroxide-blond hair—is carried to the rest of the country by the Beach Boys and Jan and Dean.

1962

The Beatles are given mop-top haircuts by Astrid Kirchherr, girlfriend of early Beatles bassist Stu Sutcliffe. Soon the group will completely abandon their greaser image, trading leather jackets for matching collarless jackets designed by London clothier D.A. Millings.

1963

Hair length serves to draw a line between generations and lifestyles. An audience member at an early Rolling Stones concert yells, "Get your hair cut!" Mick Jagger replies: "What—and look like you?"

1957

With his bow ties and horn-rimmed glasses, Buddy Holly turns nerdiness into its own form of cool. Twenty years later, Elvis Costello would do the same thing.

1964
Bouffant hairdos and glittery sequined gowns define the chic uptown look of the Supremes, Martha and the Vandellas and other Motown soul divas.

1965
The mod scene explodes in England. These kids pursue a lifestyle defined by "a real smart suit, good shoes, good shirts [and] plenty of pills," according to Pete Townshend of the Who, a band that grew out of the mod movement.

1966
A store called Granny Takes a Trip opens in London, selling psychedelic clothing to rock stars and trendsetters.

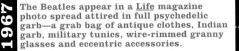

1967
The Beatles appear in a <u>Life</u> magazine photo spread attired in full psychedelic garb—a grab bag of antique clothes, Indian garb, military tunics, wire-rimmed granny glasses and eccentric accessories.

1969

West Coast rock bands like the Byrds, Creedence Clearwater Revival and the Grateful Dead dress down for the stage, attiring themselves as plainly as audience members. "We were all into blue jeans and flannel shirts," explained Chris Hillman of the Byrds.

1968

Elvis Presley emerges on his celebrated TV comeback special in a black leather outfit, reasserting his sex appeal.

1971

David Bowie wears women's dresses on his first trip to the United States, presaging a coming wave of androgyny and cross-dressing.

1972

The glitter-rock movement hits its stride as Roxy Music, the New York Dolls, T. Rex, and David Bowie and his Spiders from Mars adopt ostentatious, gender-bending stage outfits.

1973
With the emergence of Kiss, heavy-metal musicians begin turning away from jeans and t-shirts to a theatrical glam style for live performance.

1974
Designer-entrepreneurs Vivienne Westwood and Malcolm McLaren open a London clothing store called SEX, selling fetish wear and pornographic t-shirts to embryonic punk rockers. The Sex Pistols are eventually formed from the store's pool of regulars.

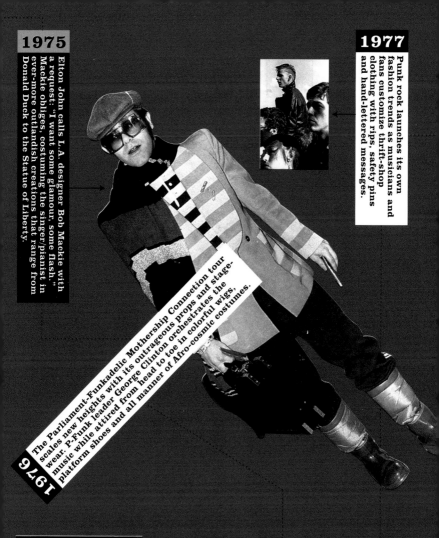

1975

Elton John calls L.A. designer Bob Mackie with a request: "I want some glamour, some flash." Mackie obliges, costuming the singer/pianist in ever-more outlandish creations that range from Donald Duck to the Statue of Liberty.

1977

Punk rock launches its own fashion trends as musicians and fans customize thrift-shop clothing with rips, safety pins and hand-lettered messages.

1976

The Parliament-Funkadelic Mothership Connection tour scales new heights with its outrageous props and stage-wear. P-Funk leader George Clinton orchestrates the music while attired from head to toe in colorful wigs, platform shoes and all manner of Afro-cosmic costumes.

1977

The film Saturday Night Fever becomes a national phenomenon. Disco music and dance-club attire—white suits, gauzy shirts with gull-wing collars—briefly enjoy broad mainstream popularity.

1979
Debbie Harry of Blondie sports a throwaway-chic look. Black clothes, red lipstick and garments fashioned from material found in dumpsters make up Harry's stage wardrobe, a camp study in trash-with-style.

1981
The new romantics movement blossoms out of London, with groups like Spandau Ballet and Duran Duran placing fashion on an equal footing with music.

1984
Prince ushers in the neo-psychedelic look with his film Purple Rain, recalling Jimi Hendrix's regal bearing with his flowing purple coat, frilly shirts and glittery bell bottoms.

1984
Bruce Springsteen's look on the cover of <u>Born in the U.S.A.</u> revives the image of the rock and roller as working-class hero. Springsteen's unpretentious uniform of red bandanna, white t-shirt and blue jeans becomes an American classic.

1986
Run-D.M.C. emerge on the rap scene with a no-nonsense look—Adidas shoes, Kangol hats and leather jackets—that is adapted straight from the streets to the stage.

1992
Bands such as Nirvana and Pearl Jam popularize the grunge look, an anti-fashion statement harking back to both dissident punks and disheveled hippies. Flannel shirts, baggy pants cut off below the knee, dyed hair or shaved heads, body-piercing and tattoos are the order of the day.

1985
In the film Desperately Seeking Susan, Madonna perfects a look that endears her to a generation of young girls. Madonna's disheveled downtown chic derives from thrift-shop scavenger hunts and is completed with piles of inexpensive bracelets and jewelry.

1988
At 50, Tina Turner is still thrilling audiences and pushing the fashion envelope with her daring short skirts, fishnet stockings and big, shaggy wigs.

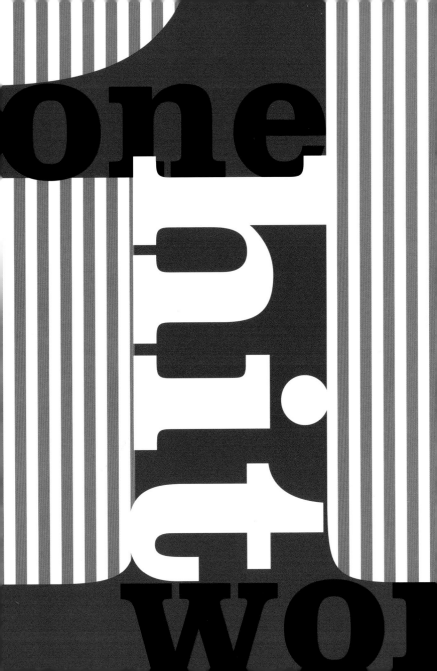

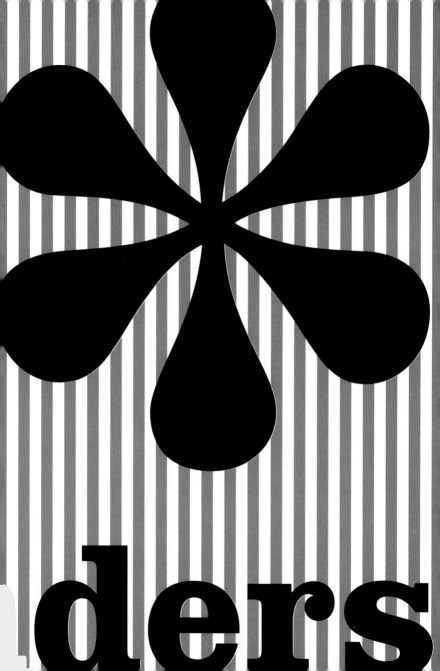

ders

One-Hit Wonders Honor Roll		
Title	Year	Band
99 Luftaballoons	1984	Nena
Afternoon Delight	1976	Starland Vocal Band
Alone	1957	The Shepherd Sisters
America	1974	Bryon MacGregor
An Open Letter to My Teenage Son	1967	Victor Lundberg
Angel Baby	1961	Rosie & the Originals
Angel in Your Arms	1977	Hot
At My Front Door	1955	The El Dorados
Baby Blue	1961	The Echoes
Barefootin'	1966	Robert Parker
Be Thankful for What You've Got	1974	William Devaughn
The Birds and the Bees	1965	Jewel Aikens
Black Betty	1977	Ram Jam
Black is Black	1966	The Bravos
Black Slacks	1957	Joe Bennett & the Sparkletones
Bobby's Girl	1962	Marcie Blane
Bongo Rock	1959	Preston Epps
Book of Love	1958	The Monotones
Born Too Late	1958	The Poni-Tails
The Boy from New York City	1965	The Ad Libs
California Sun	1964	The Rivieras
Chevy Van	1975	Sammy Johns
Chick-A-Boom (Don't Ya Jes' Love It)	1971	Daddy Dewdrop
Chirpy Chirpy Cheep Cheep	1971	Mac and Katie Kissoon
Color Him Father	1969	The Winstons
Come on Down to My Boat	1967	Every Mother's Son
Come to Me	1979	France Joli
Confidential	1956	Sonny Knight

*One-Hit Wonders For as far back as rock and roll can remember, there have been artists associated with one song–and one song only. It may have been their debut record-ing, or it may have come after an entire career's worth of show-business perseverance. Each of these songs was a Top 20 hit, and not one of the artists who recorded them ever had another song in the Top 40. If, as Andy Warhol once predict-ed, everyone is to be famous for 15 minutes, then the one-hit wonders represent rock and roll's unique fulfillment of the prophesy.

Starland Vocal Band
"Afternoon Delight"
No. 1 July 1976
I was at a bar in D.C. that had these happy appetizers–spiced shrimp, hot brie with almonds–early yuppie food. They called them Afternoon Delights. I thought to myself, Now there's a great title for a song.
–Bill Danoff, leader

Phil Phillips
"Sea of Love",
No. 2 August 1959
I was dating this girl who was always complaining I didn't love

One-Hit Wonders Honor Roll

Title	Year	Band
Cool Jerk	1966	The Capitols
Dancin' in the Moonlight	1972	King Harvest
Denise	1963	Randy & the Rainbows
Der Kommisar	1983	After the Fire
Diamonds and Pearls	1960	The Paradons
Ding Dong the Witch is Dead	1967	The Fifth Estate
Disco Duck	1976	Rick Dees & His Cast of Idiots
Doctor's Orders	1975	Carol Douglas
Dominique	1963	The Singing Nun
Double Shot of My Baby's Love	1966	The Swingin' Medallions
Down the Aisle of Love	1958	The Quintones
Earth Angel	1955	The Penguins
Eddie My Love	1956	The Teen Queens
Eighteen With a Bullet	1975	Pete Wingfield
Emotion	1978	Samantha Sang
Endless Sleep	1958	Jody Reynolds
Eres Tu (Touch the Wind)	1974	Mocedades
Everybody's Got to Learn Sometime	1980	Korgis
Everyone's Gone to the Moon	1965	Jonathan King
Farmer John	1964	The Premiers
Feelings	1975	Morris Albert
A Fifth of Beethoven	1976	Walter Murphy
Fire	1968	The Crazy World of Arthur Brown
Float On	1977	The Floaters
Friday on My Mind	1967	The Easybeats
From a Jack to a King	1963	Ned Miller
Funky Nassau	1971	Beginning of the End
Funkytown	1980	Lipps, Inc.
Get a Job	1958	The Silhouettes

1978: SAMANTHA SANG, "EMOTION" IN THE LATE SEVENTIES AND EARLY EIGHTIES, BARRY GIBB OF THE BEE GEES HELPED WRITE AND PRODUCE A NUMBER OF HITS FOR OTHER ARTISTS, INCLUDING YVONNE ELLIMAN, BARBRA STREISAND, KENNY ROGERS, DOLLY PARTON, AND GIBB SIBLING, ANDY. UNLIKE OTHER BENEFICIARIES, HOWEVER, SAMANTHA SANG HAD NEITHER PREVIOUS NOR SUBSEQUENT HITS AFTER HER BRUSH WITH THE GIBB MAGIC TOUCH.

her. One day I began thinking of a scenario where I took her out on the beach. I would show her how much I cared by taking her to a sea of love. It took about twenty minutes to write it. The gas man came to read the meter and heard me singing it. He said, "That's a wonderful song; you should do something about it."
–Phil Phillips

The Elegants
"Little Star"
No. 1 August 1958
The inspiration for "Little Star"? Sheer boredom. We'd been rehearsing all day and started to get silly, and after a while we started singing anything: poems, jingles, nursery rhymes.

We started doing "Twinkle Twinkle," and bingo—we stopped laughing. The next morning, Artie Venosa and I sat down and wrote the song.
–Vito Picone, lead singer

Joe Jeffrey Group
"My Pledge of Love"
No. 14 July 1969
I moved to Cleveland in 1964. I put together a trio and we used to play at a place called Punch

One-Hit Wonders Honor Roll

Title	Year	Band
Girl Watcher	1968	The O'Kaysions
Goin' Down	1982	Greg Guidry
Green Tambourine	1968	The Lemon Pipers
Happy, Happy Birthday, Baby	1957	The Tune Weavers
Have I the Right	1964	The Honeycombs
Hot Smoke and Sassafras	1969	Bubble Puppy
House of the Rising Sun	1970	Frijid Pink
How Do You Do	1972	Mouth and MacNeal
How Long	1975	Ace
I Love the Nightlife (Disco 'Round)	1978	Alicia Bridges
I Love You	1968	People
I'd Like to Teach the World to Sing	1972	The Hillside Singers
I'm Available	1957	Margie Rayburn
I'm Too Sexy	1992	Right Said Fred
I've Had It	1959	The Bell Notes
I've Never Been to Me	1982	Charlene
Image of a Girl	1960	The Safaris
In the Year 2525 (Exordium and Terminus)	1969	Zager & Evans
Israelites	1969	Desmond Dekker & the Aces
Judy in Disguise (With Glasses)	1968	John Fred & His Playboy Band
Junk Food Junkie	1976	Larry Groce
Just Like Romeo and Juliet	1964	The Reflections
Just One Look	1963	Doris Troy
Just When I Needed You Most	1979	Randy Vanwarmer
Key Largo	1982	Bertie Higgins
Killer Joe	1963	Rocky Fellers
Kung Fu Fighting	1974	Carl Douglas
Let It All Hang Out	1967	The Hombres
Let Me In	1962	The Sensations

1975. ACE, "HOW LONG": THE BAND ACE MAY HAVE BEEN A BLIP ON THE CHARTS, BUT THEIR LEAD SINGER PAUL CARRACK WENT ON TO BIGGER AND BETTER THINGS. IN THE EIGHTIES HE BECAME THE KEYBOARDIST FOR SQUEEZE AND SANG LEAD ON THEIR CLASSIC "TEMPTED." IN THE NINETIES, HE WAS A VOCALIST FOR MIKE AND THE MECHANICS AND CAN BE HEARD ON THEIR HUGE HIT "THE LIVING YEARS."

1963. DORIS TROY, "JUST ONE LOOK": DORIS TROY WAS ONE OF THE LUCKY FEW (ALONG WITH JAMES TAYLOR) TO HAVE AN ALBUM RELEASED ON THE BEATLES' APPLE LABEL. SHE LATER BECAME THE INSPIRATION FOR THE POPULAR BLACK MUSICAL MAMMA, I WANT TO SING.

and Judy's. One night I started playing some chords on the guitar, and this song came into my head: "My Pledge of Love." The audience went crazy. A producer heard me and asked if I wanted to record it. I said, "Oh, I don't care. Sure." See, I'd made recordings before, but nothing I did ever got off the shelf. Months went by and it didn't seem like anything was going to happen. Then one day we were driving to Buffalo, New York, for a show and suddenly the song came on the radio. The deejay said it was 25 with a bullet. I'll tell you, it shook me up! I got out of the car and was screaming; My buddy said, "Hey man, that's us!" We were dancing on the side of the road; it was beautiful.

–Joe Jeffrey

Rosie and the Originals
"Angel Baby"
No. 5 January 1961

We didn't know anything about making records. I had a cold, the band kept making mistakes, and to top it off, the horn player couldn't come because his mom made him stay home to clean the yard; so the bass player had to do the saxophone part.
–Rosie Hamlin, lead singer

The Bubble Puppy
"Hot Smoke and Sassafras"
No. 14 April 1969

We got our name from the Aldous Huxley novel, Brave New World. There's a futuristic chil- dren's game in it called Centrifu- gal Bumble Puppy. One night, probably when we were on acid, that somehow became Bubble Puppy. Our favorite place to play was a club in Houston. We had this great piece of music–we jammed all the time–and were searching for some words. One night, we're watching The

One-Hit Wonders Honor Roll		
Title	Year	Band
Liar, Liar	1965	The Castaways
Lies	1966	The Knickerbockers
Little Arrows	1968	Leapy Lee
A Little Bit of Soap	1961	The Jarmels
A Little Bit of Soul	1967	Music Explosion
Little Girl	1966	Syndicate of Sound
Little Star	1958	The Elegants
The Lord's Prayer	1974	Sister Janet Mead
Love Can Make You Happy	1969	Mercy
Love Jones	1972	Brighter Side of Darkness
Magic	1975	Pilot
Mama Didn't Lie	1963	Jan Bradley
Maniac	1983	Michael Sembello
Mickey	1982	Toni Basil
A Million to One	1960	Jimmy Charles
Montego Bay	1970	Bobby Bloom
Mother-in-Law	1961	Ernie K-Doe
Motorcycle Mama	1972	Sailcat
Mr. Custer	1960	Larry Verne
Mr. Lee	1957	The Bobbettes
Muleskinner Blues	1960	The Fendermen
My Maria	1973	B.W. Stephenson
My Pledge of Love	1969	The Joe Jeffrey Group
Na Na Hey Hey Kiss Him Goodbye	1969	Steam
The Night Chicago Died	1974	Paper Lace
Nobody But Me	1968	Human Beinz
Oh, Babe, What Would You Say	1972	Hurricane Smith
Oh Happy Day	1969	Edwin Hawkins Singers
Oh Julie	1958	The Crescendos

1963: JAN BRADLEY, "MAMA DIDN'T LIE" JAN BRADLEY WAS ONLY NINETEEN WHEN HER SOLE HIT MADE THE CHARTS. "MAMA DIDN'T LIE" DIDN'T MAKE HER A LASTING STAR, BUT THE SONG LIVED ON IN THE SOUNDTRACK OF JOHN WATERS'S FILM *HAIRSPRAY*—HIS HOMAGE TO SIXTIES R&B.

1972: HURRICANE SMITH, "OH, BABE, WHAT WOULD YOU SAY" NORMAN "HURRICANE" SMITH WAS ORIGINALLY A NOTED SOUND-STUDIO ENGINEER BEFORE HIS CAMPY BRUSH WITH FAME. HE WORKED IN THE STUDIO WITH BOTH THE BEATLES AND PINK FLOYD.

One-Hit Wonders Honor Roll		
Title	Year	Band
One Summer Night	1958	The Danleers
Over the Mountain	1957	Johnnie & Joe
Pac-Man Fever	1982	Buckner & Garcia
Party Lights	1962	Claudine Clark
Pass the Dutchie	1983	Musical Youth
Penetration	1964	The Pyramids
Pipeline	1963	The Chantays
Play That Funky Music	1976	Wild Cherry
Playground in My Mind	1973	Clint Holmes
Pledging My Love	1955	Johnny Ace
Pop Music	1979	M
Popcorn	1972	Hot Butter
Popsicles and Icicles	1965	The Murmaids
Priscilla	1956	Eddie Cooley & the Dimples
Psychotic Reaction	1966	Count Five
Put Your Hand in the Hand	1971	Ocean
Puttin' on the Ritz	1983	Taco
Reach Out of the Darkness	1968	Friend and Lover
Reflections of My Life	1970	Marmalade
Rhythm of the Rain	1963	The Cascades
Ring My Bell	1979	Anita Ward
Sally, Go 'Round the Roses	1963	The Jaynetts
Sea Cruise	1959	Frankie Ford
Sea of Love	1959	Phil Phillips
Smoky Places	1962	The Corsairs
So Fine	1959	The Fiestas
Sorry (I Ran All the Way Home)	1959	The Impalas
Spirit in the Sky	1970	Norman Greenbaum
Sukiyaki	1963	Kyu Sakamoto

Beverly Hillbillies, and Granny goes, "Hot smoke and sassafras, Jethro!" That's all we needed.
–David Fore, drummer

Friend and Lover
"Reach out of the Darkness"
No. 10 June 1968
The inspiration for the song came after I went to a love-in in New York City. I wrote three separate pieces of music–just choruses and refrains, no verses– and I realized they somehow fit together.

Cathy (Conn) and I went to Verve Records and the man there said, "You have to give me a tape. I don't like to hear music in person. You're a couple of cute kids and I could make a mistake." I said, "Okay, turn your chair around and look out the window while we sing." It worked.

They had a selective service sit-in in San Francisco. Someone took a sound truck and started playing the song on the street, and it became an overnight hit.
–Jim Post, friend

Lipps, Inc.
"Funkytown"
No. 1 May 1980
I went to a promotion meeting. The black-music guy said, "We'll

never get it on black radio–too much synthesizer." The pop guy said, "Too black, not pop enough." The disco guy said, "Disco's waning; it won't make it." One of the heads of the company, who weighed 350 pounds, got up and said, "This song is a smash hit, and if you don't get it played, I'll sit on all of you." It went from 66 to 10 on the dance charts in one week.

–Steve Greenberg, songwriter and producer

Joe Bennett and the Sparkletones
"Black Slacks"
No. 17 October 1957

After "Black Slacks" hit, we were out to Las Vegas and played there, too. Elvis came to see us, and they brought him backstage after our set. The first thing he said was, "Where'd you get those jackets?"

–Joe Bennett, lead guitar and vocalist

1966: NAPOLEON XIV, "THEY'RE COMING TO TAKE ME AWAY" NAPOLEON XIV'S BRIEF MOMENT IN THE CHARTS WAS MADE EVEN BRIEFER AFTER HIS GLEEFULLY UN-PC ODE TO INSANITY WAS DEEMED OFFENSIVE TO THE MENTALLY ILL AND WAS QUICKLY BANNED THROUGHOUT THE COUNTRY. THE SINGLE'S FLIPSIDE WAS THE SAME SONG PLAYED BACKWARDS.

1977: DEBBY BOONE, "YOU LIGHT UP MY LIFE" DEBBY BOONE, PAT BOONE'S DAUGHTER, HAD ONLY ONE HIT, BUT IT WAS A BIG ONE. "YOU LIGHT UP MY LIFE" WAS NUMBER ONE FOR TEN CONSECUTIVE WEEKS AND HELPED WIN BOONE A GRAMMY FOR BEST NEW ARTIST.

One-Hit Wonders Honor Roll

Title	Year	Band
Susie Darlin'	1958	Robin Luke
Talk Talk	1967	Music Machine
Teen Angel	1960	Mark Dinning
Telephone Man	1977	Meri Wilson
Telstar	1962	The Tornadoes
Then You Can Tell Me Goodbye	1967	The Casinos
There's a Moon Out Tonight	1961	The Capris
They're Coming to Take Me Away, Ha-Haa!	1966	Napoleon XIV
Thunder and Lightning	1972	Chi Coltrane
Tie Me Kangaroo Down, Sport	1963	Rolf Harris
Timothy	1971	The Buoys
Tired of Toein' the Line	1980	Rocky Burnette
Toast and Marmalade for Tea	1971	Tin Tin
Too Shy	1983	Kajagoogoo
Torture	1962	Kris Jensen
Tragedy	1959	Thomas Wayne
Turn the Beat Around	1976	Vickie Sue Robinson
Uh! Oh!	1959	The Nutty Squirrels
Undercover Angel	1977	Alan O'Day
Venus	1970	Shocking Blue
Volare	1958	Domenico Modugno
Walking on Sunshine	1985	Katrina & the Waves
What Kind of Fool	1963	The Tams
When We Get Married	1962	Ronnie & the Hi-Lites
Wonderful Summer	1963	Robin Ward
You Cheated	1958	The Shields
You Light Up My Life	1977	Debby Boone
You Turn Me On	1965	Ian Whitcomb
Your Wild Heart	1957	Joy Layne

Legends
of the
Airwaves
and
Rock Goes to the Movies

"Music,

If
Call
You
If'

k
the
Pages
lia
Back
My

My Back Pages

Sixties

Prior to the mid-sixties, rock journalism, whether in daily newspapers or in magazines like *16* and *Hit Parader*, was oriented toward young teens. Their focus was on the length of a performer's hair, rather than the power of his music. The few exceptions, such as *Sing Out* and *Little Sandy Review*, were devoted mainly to folk music. But as rock and roll became more urgent, rebellious and political, a new generation of journalists began to explore the music and its meanings, giving birth to publications such as San Francisco's *Mojo Navigator*, Boston's *Crawdaddy* and Detroit's *Creem*.

Founded in 1967 by Jann Wenner, *Rolling Stone* became the first significant publication that understood the tremendous importance and impact of rock and roll on society. Featuring the work of such respected writers as Hunter S. Thompson, Tom Wolfe, Joe Eszterhas, Greil Marcus and Jon Landau and photographer Annie Leibovitz, the magazine broke new ground with its serious and critical approach toward music, politics and culture. Suddenly, rock and roll was a serious subject, worthy of serious critical evaluation, and rock artists found themselves the subject of in-depth interviews, in which they offered their opinions not just on music, but on the state of world affairs. At about the same time, the underground political press, defined by publications like *The Los Angeles Free Press*, the *Fifth Estate* and the *Ann Arbor Argus*, grew out of a similar desire to offer an alternative to mainstream media.

Seventies

As rock and roll evolved, so, too, did rock journalism. The early seventies brought glam-rock and glossy publications like New York's *Rock Scene*, which celebrated glam decadence and mirrored the music's flash. In the mid-seventies, punk began to explode and with it came cheaply produced do-it-yourself "zines" — among the most memorable and groundbreaking were *Sniffin' Glue*, *Punk* and *New York Rocker*.

Eighties and Nineties

With the eighties and nineties came rap, heavy metal and most important, MTV. Magazines such as *Rip*, *The Source*, *Spin*, and *Vibe* began to emerge, with a fresh graphic style that reiterated MTV's in-your-face approach to music, fashion, and sex.

Today, as alternative music has conquered the charts, once-underground publications like Cleveland's *Alternative Press* and San Diego's *Ray Gun* have moved into the mainstream, leaving critics and readers looking once again for a new music-press vanguard.

Legends of the Airwaves

Kid Leo
King of Cleveland Radio when station was national powerhouse
WMMS Cleveland
1970s–1980s

Wolfman Jack
"jive talk and wolf howls" and R&B
XERF Mexico
XERB Mexico
WNJR Newark, NJ
WYOU Newport News, VA
KCIJ Shreveport, LA
National syndication
1960s–1980s

Murray the K
Early Beatles jock
WINS New York
WOR New York
WMCA New York
1950s–1990s

Redbeard
Dallas's best known rock jock
WHMQ Findlay, OH
KFMQ Lincoln, NB
WCCC Hartford, CT
WZXR Memphis
KTXQ Dallas
1970s–1980s

Jed the Fish
KROQ Los Angeles
1970s–1990s

Symphony Sid
Jazz trumpeter turned R&B deejay
WBNX New York
WHOM New York
WMCA New York
WABC New York
WOR New York
WBMS Boston
1930s–1950s

Rosko
On-air rapper and poet
WNJR Union City, NJ
WNEW-FM New York
WOR-FM New York
WBLS New York
WKTU New York
1960s–1980s

Oedipus
New-music mold-breaker
WTBS Boston
WBCN Boston
1970s–1980s

Hoss Allen
Early R&B/gospel jock
WHIN Gallatin, TN
WLAC Nashville
1940s–1990s

Herb Oscar Anderson
Started every big-band/rock show with a hymn
WHN New York
WDGY New York
WABC New York
WMCA New York
1950s–1960s

Jack Armstrong
Rock radio's "fastest mouth in the west"
WAYS Charlotte
WIXY Cleveland
WKYC Cleveland
WKBW Buffalo
WIFE Indianapolis
1960s–1980s

Billy Bass
Pioneer of progressive Cleveland radio
WIXY Cleveland
WNCR Cleveland
WMMS Cleveland
1960s–1970s

Paul Berlin
Spread the gospel of live rock and roll to Texas
KNUZ Houston
KQUE Houston
1950s–1990s

Rodney Bigenheimer
L.A.'s best-known new-music ground-breaker
KROQ Los Angeles
1970s–1990s

Dick Biondi
One of rock radio's first bad boys
WLS Chicago
WJMK Chicago
WKBW Buffalo
WHOT Youngstown, OH
WCFL Chicago
WSAI Cincinnati
WBBM Chicago
KRLA Los Angeles
WNMB North Myrtle, SC
1950s–1990s

Jerry Blavat
Philly radio mainstay
WPGR Philadelphia
WHAT Philadelphia
WSSJ Philadelphia
1960s–1990s

Martin Block
One of the country first deejays
WNEW New York
WABC New York
WOR New York
KFWB Los Angeles
1930s–1960s

Forky Chedwick
R&B's "Daddio of the Radio"
WAMO Pittsburgh
1950s–1980s

Dick Clark
rock's most recognized voice and face
WFIL Philadelphia
1950s

Tom Clay
WJBK Detroit
WSAI Cincinnati
KDAY Los Angeles
WPPC Los Angeles
KQQ Los Angeles
KZLA Los Angeles
1950s–1970s

Al "Jazzbeaux" Collins
WNEW New York
KSFO San Francisco
KFI Los Angeles
WJAS Pittsburgh
WIND Chicago
1940s–1980s

Frankie Crocker
WBLS New York
WMCA New York
1960s–1970s

Steve Dahl
"Disco Demolition" early shock jock
WLUP Chicago
WABX Detroit
WWWW Detroit
WBR Chicago
WLS-AM Chicago
WLUP-AM Chicago
1970s–1990s

Bobby Dale
One of the first top-40 deejays
KDWB Minneapolis
KEWB Los Angeles
KEWB Oakland
KRLA Los Angeles
KFRC San Francisco
KSFO San Francisco
KYCY San Francisco
1960s–1990s

Yvonne Daniels
"The First Lady of Chicago Radio"
WYNR Chicago
WCFL Chicago
WSDM Chicago
WLS Chicago
WVON Chicago
WNUA Chicago
1960s–1980s

Rick Dees
King of L.A. pop and recorder of "Disco Duck"
WMPS Memphis
KHJ Los Angeles
KIIS Los Angeles
1970s–1980s

Doctor Demento
Favorite spinner of rock rarities
KPPC Los Angeles
National syndication
1970s–1990s

Tom Donahue
Father of FM progressive radio
WINX Rockville, MD
WTIP Charleston, SC
WIBG Philadelphia
KYA San Francisco
KMPX San Francisco
KSAN San Francisco
1950s–1970s

Rachel Donahue
KMPX San Francisco
KSAN San Francisco
KLIS Los Angeles
KROQ Los Angeles
KMET Los Angeles
KWST Los Angeles
MARS Los Angeles
1960s–1990s

Dale Dorman
Boston radio's "Uncle Dale"
WOLF Syracuse
WRKO Boston
WXKS Boston
1960s–1990s

Lavada "Dr. Hepcat" Durst
One of Texas's first black deejays
KVET Austin
1940s–1960s

Kenny Everett
Early controversial voice on pirate radio
Radio London (Pirate)
BBC Radio One London
Capitol Radio London
BBC Radio Two London
Capitol Gold London
1960s–1990s

Max Floyd
KYYS Kansas City
KLZ Denver
1970s–1990s

Alan Freed
Early godfather of rock and roll radio
WAKR Akron, OH
WJW Cleveland
WINS New York
WABC New York
KDAY Los Angeles
1940s–1960s

Alan "Fluff" Freeman
Father of "Pick of the Pops"
Radio Luxembourg
BBC One London

Capitol Radio London
Capitol Gold London
1950s–1990s

Jack "The Rapper" Gibson
Helped start the first black-owned station
WERD Atlanta
WLOU Louisville
WMBM Miami
WCIN Cincinnati
WABQ Cleveland
1940s–1950s

Charlie Gillett
London jock and music historian
BBC Radio London
GLR London
1970s–1990s

Arnie "Woo Woo" Ginsberg
WMEX Boston
WBOS Boston
WRKO Boston
WXKS Boston
1950s–1960s

Hunter Hancock
Legendary spinner of beebob, swing, blues, and boogie
KFVD Los Angeles
KPOP Los Angeles
KGBF Los Angeles

KGFJ Los Angeles
1950s–1960s

Harry Harrison
Veteran morning jock
WMCA New York
WABC New York
WCBS New York
1950s–1990s

Terri Hemmert
Die-hard Beatles fan and prog rock deejay
WXRT Chicago
WGLD Chicago
WCMF Rochester
1960s–1990s

Douglas "Jocko" Henderson
New York and Philly's early "rhythm talker"
WDAS Philadelphia
WSID Baltimore
WLIB New York
WADO New York
WCBS New York
1950s–1960s

Dave Herman
New York's champion of rock radio
WNEW New York
WXRK New York
WABC New York
WMMR Philadelphia
1960s–1990s

Maurice "Hot Rod" Hulbert
WDIA Memphis
WITH Baltimore
WHAT Philadelphia
WWRL New York
WEBB Baltimore
WWIN Baltimore
1940s–1950s

Dan Ingram
"The thinking man's deejay"
WABC New York
WCBS New York
WNHC New Haven, CT
WIL St. Louis
KBOX Denver
1960s–1990s

Hal Jackson
WOOK Wash., D.C.
WINX Wash., D.C.
WSID Baltimore
WANN Annapolis, MD
WMCA New York
WNJR New York
WABC New York
WLIB New York
WBLS New York
1940s–1990s

Casey Kasem
Syndicated sensation and father of "America's Top 40"
WJBK Detroit
WJW Cleveland

KEWB Oakland
KRLA Los Angeles
National Syndication
1950s–1990s

Russ "Weird Beard" Knight
Master of the high-energy radio show
KLIF Dallas
WXYZ Detroit
WHK Cleveland
KILT Houston
KBOX Denver
KLZ Denver
WAKR Akron, OH
WNEW-AM New York
1960s–1980s

Art Laboe
Veteran oldies spinner
KXLA Los Angeles
KPOP Los Angeles
KPPC Los Angeles
KRTH Los Angeles
KRLA Los Angeles
1950s–1990s

Jim Ladd
Progressive FM innovator
KMET Los Angeles
KLOS Los Angeles
KNAC Long Beach, CA
KLSX Los Angeles
1960s–1990s

John "Records" Landecker
Classic rocker and master of call-in madness
WJMK Chicago
WLS Chicago
WLUP Chicago
WCKG Chicago
CFTR Toronto
WIBG Philadelphia
1970s–1990s

Charles Laquidara
Pioneer of underground and free-form radio
WBCN Boston
KPPC Los Angeles
1960s–1990s

Hy Lit
R&B jock—"on the scene with the record machine"
WIBG Philadelphia
WHAT Philadelphia
WDAS Philadelphia
WPGR Philadelphia
WOGL Philadelphia
WCAU Philadelphia
1950s–1990s

George "Hound Dog" Lorenz
Early rock and roll pioneer
WKBW Buffalo
WBTA Batavia, NY
WXRA Buffalo
WJJL Niagara, NY
WSRS Cleveland
WBLK Buffalo
1940s–1960s

Larry Lujack
One of the Windy City's most loved deejays
WLS Chicago
WCFL Chicago
KJR Seattle
1960s–1980s

Ron Lundy
WHMM Memphis
WDDT Greenville, MS
WLCS Baton Rouge
WIL St. Louis
WABC New York
WCBS-FM New York
1950s–1990s

Dave Marsden
Early promoter of alternative rock format
CKEY Toronto
CHOM-FM Toronto
CHUM Toronto
CFNY Toronto
1960s–1980s

Brian Matthew
Radio Luxembourg
BBC Radio One London
1940s–1990s

Sonny Melendrez
KTSA San Antonio
KELP El Paso
KINT El Paso
KMPC Los Angeles
KRLA Los Angeles
KISS Los Angeles
KFI Los Angeles
KTFM San Antonio
KSMG San Antonio
1960s–1990s

"Humble Harve" Miller
One of the first to put "The Twist" on the air
WIBG Philadelphia
WHAT Philadelphia
WMID Atlantic City
KBLA Los Angeles
KHJ Los Angeles
K-EARTH Los Angeles
KRLA Los Angeles
1960s–1990s

Carol Miller
Standard-bearer of classic-rock radio
WPLJ New York
WQIV New York
WNEW New York
WMMR Philadelphia
1970s–1990s

Bob Mitchell
Talk show host turned Top 40 jock
WIBG Philadelphia
WMID Atlantic City
WPEN Philadelphia
KYA San Francisco
KHJ Los Angeles
1950s–1960s

Magnificent Montague
KGFJ Los Angeles
XERB Mexico
XPRS Mexico
1960s

Robert W. Morgan
L.A.'s morning "Boss Jock"
KRTH Los Angeles
KHJ Los Angeles
KMPC Los Angeles
KEWB San Francisco
1960s–1990s

Bruce "Cousin Brucie" Morrow
WABC New York
WINS New York
WNBC New York
WCBS New York
1950s–1990s

Scott Muni
Dubbed "The Professor" of cutting-edge music
WAKR Akron, OH
WABC New York
WMCA New York
WOR New York
WNEW New York
1950s–1990s

Pete "Mad Daddy" Myers
WHK Cleveland
WJW Cleveland
WNEW New York
WINS New York
1950s–1960s

Danny Neaverth
Buffalo's favorite jock for 35 years
WBNY Buffalo
WKBW Buffalo
WHTT Buffalo
1960s–1990s

Jay Nelson
WKBW Buffalo
CHUM Toronto
1960s–1980s

Joe "Rockin' Bird" Niagara
Long-lived classics/standards spinner
WIBG Philadelphia
WDAS Philadelphia
WCAU Philadelphia
WPEN Philadelphia
1940s–1990s

Annie Nightingale
UK's first female deejay
BBC Radio One London
1970s–1990s

Gene Nobles
Early host of late-night "dance hours"
WLAC Nashville
1940s–1970s

Pat O'Day
KJR Seattle
1950s–1970s

Mark Parenteau
WBCN Boston
WABX Detroit
1960s–1990s

Arthur Penhallow
"The Grand Poobah" of Detroit rock radio
WRIF Detroit
1970s–1980s

Dewey Phillips
WHBQ Memphis
1940s–1950s

Jimmy Rabbitt
KLIF Dallas
KCBQ San Diego
KRLA Los Angeles
KMET Los Angeles
KHJ Los Angeles
KROQ Los Angeles
1960s–1980s

Johnny Rabbitt
KXOK St. Louis
WIL St. Louis
KSHE St. Louis
KADI St. Louis
WRTH St. Louis
1960s–1990s

B. Mitchell Reed
Made successful move
from jazz to progres-
sive rock
WOR New York
WINS New York
WMCA New York
KFWB Los Angeles
KRLA Los Angeles
KPPC Los Angeles
KMET Los Angeles
KLOS Los Angeles
1950s–1980s

Joey Reynolds
WKBW Buffalo
WPOP Hartford, CT
WDRC Hartford, CT
WIXY Cleveland
WXYZ Detroit
WIBG Philadelphia
KMPC Los Angeles
KRTH Los Angeles
WFIL Philadelphia
WNBC New York
WPLG Miami
WIOD Miami
1960s–1990s

**"John R."
Richbourg**
Pioneering soul deejay
WLAC Nashville
1940s–1970s

Red Robinson
Credited as first to put
rock and roll on air in
Canada
CJOR Vancouver
CKWX Vancouver
CFUN Vancouver
CKNW Vancouver
CISL Vancouver
KGW Portland
1950s–1990s

"Doctor" Don Rose
KFRC San Francisco
WFIL Philadelphia
WQXI Atlanta
KWMT Fort Dodge, IA
KOIL Omaha, NB
KTSA San Antonio
1960s–1980s

Emperor Rosko
One of Europe's best
known deejays
Radio Caroline London
Radio Luxembourg
Radio Swiss Geneva
BBC London
1960s–1970s

Denny Sanders
Cleveland radio main-
stay for eclectic rock
WBCN Boston
WTBS Cambridge
WMMS Cleveland
WMJI Cleveland
1960s–1990s

Maxanne Sartori
WBCN Boston
WNEW New York
KOL-FM Seattle
WBOS Boston
KEZX Seattle
KJET Seattle
KZOK Seattle
KMBY Monterey, CA
1970s–1980s

**Zenas "Daddy"
Sears**
R&B deejay and rights
activist
WGST Atlanta
WAOK Atlanta
1940s–1960s

Robin Seymour
Favorite pop jock of
60s Detroit teens
WKMH Detroit
WKNR Detroit
CKLW Detroit
1940s–1960s

Scott Shannon
First voice of the
"Morning Zoo" format
WABB Mobile, AL
WMAK Nashville
WPGC Wash., D.C.
Q105 Tampa
Z100 New York
WPLJ New York
WQXI Atlanta
Pirate Radio,
Los Angeles
1970s–1990s

Don Sherwood
KSFO San Francisco
KROW San Francisco
KCBS San Francisco
1940s–1970s

**Dave "The Duke"
Sholin**
Frisco's Top 40 expert
KFRC San Francisco
KLIV San Jose
1970s–1990s

Bonnie Simmons
Bay area's voice for
eclectic rock
KSAN San Francisco
KFOG San Francisco
KOFY-FM San Francisco
LIVE 105 San Francisco
KPFA Berkeley
KUSF San Francisco
1970s–1990s

**"The Real" Don
Steele**
KHJ Los Angeles
K-EARTH Los Angeles
KRLA Los Angeles
KIQQ Los Angeles
KTNQ Los Angeles
KCBS Los Angeles
1960s–1990s

**Alison "The
Nightbird" Steele**
Female radio pioneer
and prog rock specialist
WNEW New York
WXRK New York
1960s–1990s

**Martha Jean
"The Queen"
Steinberg**
WDIA Memphis
WCHB Inkster, MI
WJLB Detroit
WQBH Detroit
1950s–1990s

Sly Stone
On-air expert on SF
scene turned 60s
music legend
KSOL San Francisco
KDIA Oakland
1960s

Dusty Street
Groundbreaker for
early FM radio
KMPX San Francisco
KSAN San Francisco
KSFX San Francisco
KTIM San Rafael, CA
KROQ Los Angeles
KVST Los Angeles
KLST Los Angeles
1960s–1990s

Rufus Thomas
"The Daddy of
Memphis Soul"
WDIA Memphis
1950s–1990s

Mary Turner
KMET Los Angeles
KSAN San Francisco
1970s–1990s

Nat D. Williams
WDIA Memphis
1940s–1970s

Georgie Woods
Philly hit-breaker and
R&B promoter
WDAS Philadelphia
WHAT Philadelphia
WERL New York
WNWR Philadelphia
1950s–1990s

"If You Call It Music"

"The quality of music is poor, it really is. It brings out the **savage in people**." —disc jockey from Louisville, KY, 1953

"The screaming is mostly that R&B is driving our young people to some unwholesome passion. We are being told that this is a **narcotic on wax** that is taking them from the path of righteousness to the highways of iniquity." —Ruth Cage, April

"... poor music, badly recorded, with lyrics that are at best in poor taste and at worse obscene ... this trend in music (and **I apologize for calling it 'music'**) is affecting the ideas and lives of our children." —Bob Haymes, NY disc jockey, 1955

Bob Haymes

1955 issue of *beat*

"Elvis, who rotates his pelvis, was **appalling musically**. Also ... an exhibition that was suggestive and vulgar, tinged with the kind of animalism that should be confined to dive and bordellos." —Ben Gross, *The New York Daily News*, 1957

"**We do not like** [rock and roll] to move anybody in any spectacular way. ... At best rock and roll is a kind of **glorified hillbilly music** with a two-beat, the familiar twanging guitar, and a grotesquely distorted vocal line picked up from the blues." —editorial in *Musical/America*, 1957

Musical America

"Rock and roll ... sign of the depersonalization of the individual, of ecstatic veneration of mental decline and passivity. If we cannot stem the tide with its waves of rhythmic narcosis and of future waves of vicarious craze, **we are preparing our own downfall** in the midst of pandemic funeral dances." —Dr. Joost A. M. Meerlo, psychologist, *New York Times*, February 1957

New York Times

"Either rock and roll actually stirs them to **orgies of sex and violence** (as its model did for the savages themselves), or they use it as an excuse for the removing of all inhibitions and the complete disregard for the conventions of decency ... it has proved itself definitely a menace to youthful morals and an incitement to juvenile delinquency." —*Music Journal*, February 1958

"When you call it music, **if you call it** it music, that is anything but wholesome is forced onto them at that age, I think it is the worst possible service that the medium could be used for." —Sen. Oren Harris, Arkansas, March 1958, referring to the radio broadcast of rock and roll

Sen. Oren Harris

"**Smash the records you possess** which present a pagan culture and a pagan concept of life. Phone or write a disc jockey who is ...shing a lousy record. Switch your radio dial when you hear a suggestive song. Some songwriters need a good swift kick. So do some disk jockeys." —Catholic Youth Center, Minneapolis, 1958

"A serious warning must be sounded that the rock and roll concerts at New York's Carnegie Hall are turning into **maniac demonstrations** that are seriously endangering the lives and limbs of the teenage fans ..." —*Variety*, 1964

Variety

"There is no doubt that, in any poll for **the best-hated man** in Britain taken among people over forty, Mr. Jagger would be near the top." —*London Times*, 1965

London Times

...e Beatles and ...sands like them ...ave loosed a verit...le flood of musical trash on a generation of young Americans... Most parents seem blissfully unaware of his musical turn to insanity. But other parents have been shocked to see their daughters charged in a state of hypnotic frenzy, clutching at the long-haired slobs who twang, screech and thump in a **mixture of unrelated noise that would insult the ear of any self-respecting orangutan.**" —John Birch Society, 1966

John Birch Society

"The pop music biz is now facing its proudest 'moral crisis' since Elvis Presley outraged its elders by swiveling his hips on television some ten years ago. Compared to what's happening in pop songs today, Presley's gyrations may be considered **a model of decorum**." —June 8, 1966 issue of *Variety*

"It is repulsive to right-thinking people and can have serious effects in our young people." —J. Edgar Hoover, c. 1968

"Some [rock and roll songs] absolutely make permissible, if not encourage, **fornication** and all varieties of things that would have been called **immoral** 20 years ago." —Gordon McLendon, radio station owner, *Time* magazine, 1967

J. Edgar Hoover

"Actually, the idea that rock is **Fascism spelled Fashion** is as familiar as the fact that smoking causes cancer." —Albert Goldman, *New York Times*, November 23, 1969

"Rock utilizes brainwashing techniques and is definitely designed to delude American youth into taking drugs, participating in permissive sex activities and supporting anti-American concepts." —Joseph Crow (an expert on musical subversion), quoted in *American Opinion*, a publication of the John Birch Society, 1969

Joseph Crow

"Those rock 'festivals' are really death traps. Isn't it about time **we normal Americans** outlawed these damnable 'rock festivals'? These deafening, dope-ridden, degenerate mob scenes have no more place in our America than would a publicly promoted gang rape or legally sanctioned performance of the Black Mass ..." —1970 newspaper article

"Well, the record companies and the rock groups accomplished their purpose: **they got rich killing kids**." —Helen Keane, record producer, about rock's promotion of drug use, in *High Fidelity*, February 1970

Helen Keane

"Rock and roll is one of the 'weapons' that revolutionaries are using to tear down everything that Christianity has built up in the United States of America. Rock Music is **the devil's masterpiece** for enslaving his own children." —Frank Garlock, 1971

"I can't recall any comparable example of sustained and **uniform nonsense** in this century." —Caskie Stinett, *Atlantic Monthly*, August 1977

"The children have as their heroes banal, drug- and sex-ridden **guttersnipes** who foment rebellion not only against parents but against all noble sentiments." —Allan Bloom, *Wall Street Journal*, 1983

Allan Bloom

"[Heavy Metal] is sick and **repulsive** and **horrible** and **dangerous**." —Jeff R. Steele, Baptist minister, *Billboard*, 1984

"The First Amendment should not apply to rock and roll." —San Antonio councilman, 1985

"I'm a fairly with-it person, but this stuff is **curling my hair**." —Tipper Gore, Commerce Committee hearings September 1985

Tipper Gore

"By God, rescue the tender young ears of this nation from this—**this rock porn** ...It's outrageous filth and we've got to do something about it." —Senator Ernest Hollings, Commerce Committee hearings, *Rolling Stone*, November 7, 1985

"We should be deeply concerned about the obvious cumulative effect of this cult of violence that has captured the public's imagination and pervaded our society. Few parents realize how much the angry brand of music that is part of it [heavy metal] has presented suicide, glorified rape, and condoned murder. The message is **more than repulsive—it's deadly**." —Tipper Gore, *Raising PG Kids in an X-rated Society*, 1987

Dick Rowe

"Guitar groups are on the way out." —Dick Rowe, Decca A&R executive, on first declining the Beatles a recording contract, 1962

Rock goes to the Movies.

...And so do the stars. Some rock legends pick their favorite rock flicks.

JOE WALSH
Bye Bye Birdie
"My favorite rock and roll film was *Bye Bye Birdie*...he was, after all, the first rock star."

LOU REED
Blackboard Jungle
"First rock and roll movie seen: *Blackboard Jungle*. Attitude more than musical."
TAMI Show
"Viewer on acid. Sublime."
The Harder They Come
"Probably the all-time best and had it been rock as opposed to reggae, I would have awarded it the gold shield."
This Is Spinal Tap
"And #1, all-timer, not to be missed, must viewing on any bus tour—*This Is Spinal Tap*."

THE EDGE
Don't Look Back

DEBORAH HARRY
Tapeheads

JACKSON BROWNE
The Blues According to Lightning Hopkins

ALICE COOPER
West Side Story
"Being from Detroit, I always related to gang mentality. The original Alice Cooper band was very influenced by the *West Side Story* soundtrack—all you have to do is listen to the *School's Out* album to figure that one out. Also, some of the choreographed violence that we did onstage was inspired by the rumble scene. This movie is the essence of cool."

BOOTSY COLLINS
Wayne's World
"It reminds me of when I first started playing in the wine bars and getting paid beer to go. Those were the days."

PATTI SMITH
One Plus One

JERRY LEE LEWIS
Tobacco Road

GEORGE CLINTON
Yellow Submarine
"I saw the colors through my color blindness."

ANNIE LENNOX
This Is Spinal Tap

BILLY GIBBONS
The Harder They Come/ Blow Up
"I have two favorite rock and roll movies...*The Harder They Come*, for the grit of Jamaican realism, and *Blow Up*, for the glitz of rock-and-roll surrealism."

DUSTY HILL
King Creole
"*King Creole* is my favorite rock and roll movie because the setting is New Orleans, and it has probably the best Elvis songs of any of his movies. Also, it is good to see Walter Matthau play a bad guy."

FRANK BEARD
Eddie and the Cruisers
"I agree with Eddie: if you can't be great, why do it at all."

We also recommend:

1
A Hard Day's Night
1964. b&w, 85 min. Director: Richard Lester. Cast: the Beatles, Wilfred Brambell, Victor Spinetti, Anna Quayle. A day in the life. Comic, delightful.

2
Don't Look Back
1967. b&w, 96 min. Director: D. A. Pennebaker. Cast: Bob Dylan, Joan Baez, Donovan, Alan Price. A camera follows a young Bob Dylan on his first British tour in 1965.

3
This is Spinal Tap
1984, 82 min. Director: Rob Reiner. Cast: Michael McKean, Christopher Guest, Harry Shearer, Rob Reiner. Mock rockumentary, heavy-metal rockers.

4
The Great Rock n' Roll Swindle
1980, 104 min. Director: Julien Temple. Cast: The Sex Pistols, Malcolm McLaren. A self-conscious portrait of Britain's most notorious generators of bad publicity.

5
Gimme Shelter
1970, 91 min. Director: David Maysles, Albert Maysles, Charlotte Zwerin. Cast: The Rolling Stones, Melvin Belli. 1969 Stones concert at Altamont marred by a deadly Hell's Angels melee—the sixties are over.

6
Purple Rain
1984, 113 min. Director: Albert Magnoli. Cast: Prince, Apollonia, Morris Day, Olga Karlatos. Quest for self-awareness, love, and fame.

7
Jailhouse Rock
1957. b&w, 96 min. Director: Richard Thorpe. Cast: Elvis Presley, Mickey Shaughnessy, Dean Jones, Judy Tyler. Back in the slammer. Forget the plot; enjoy the songs.

8
The Girl Can't Help It
1957, 99 min. Director: Frank Tashlin. Cast: Tom Ewell, Jayne Mansfield, Edmond O'Brien, Julie London, Henry Jones, Fats Domino, the Platters, the Treniers, Little Richard, Gene Vincent and His Blue Caps, Eddie Cochran, Barry Gordon, Ray Anthony, Nino Tempo, the Chuckles. Mansfield vehicle chock full of early rock hits.

9
The Harder They Come
1973, 98 min. Director: Perry Henzell. Cast: Jimmy Cliff, Janet Barkley. Aspiring musician, exploited in the big city. Cult classic.

10
Wild Style
1982. Director: Charlie Ahearn. Cast: Lee Quinones, Sandra "Pink" Fabara, Fred "Fab Five Freddy" Brathwaite, Patti Astor, Busy Bee, and Grandmaster Flash. Stylized portrait of early rap and hip-hop.

And among the best performance flicks:

1
Woodstock
1970, 184 min. Director: Michael Wadleigh. Cast: Joan Baez, Canned Heat, Joe Cocker, Country Joe & the Fish, Crosby, Stills, Nash & Young, Arlo Guthrie, Richie Havens, Jimi Hendrix, Santana, John Sebastian, Sha-Na-Na, Sly & the Family Stone, Ten Years After, the Who and one-half million bands. Sixties counterculture, ultimate festival film.

2
Stop Making Sense
1984, 99 min. Director: Jonathan Demme. Cast: The Talking Heads. Conceived for the stage by David Byrne. One of the most brilliantly shot concert films ever.

3
Monterey Pop
1969, 72 min. Director: D. A. Pennebaker. Cast: Jimi Hendrix, Otis Redding, the Who, Eric Burdon and the Animals, Jefferson Airplane, Janis Joplin, Country Joe and the Fish, Canned Heat, Simon & Garfunkel, the Mamas and the Papas, Ravi Shankar. Summer of Love, 1967, the first great rock festival.

4
The Last Waltz
1978, 117 min. Director: Martin Scorsese. Cast: The Band, Bob Dylan, Neil Young, Joni Mitchell, Van Morrison, Eric Clapton, Neil Diamond, Muddy Waters. The Band's celebratory swan song.

5
Rolling Stones at the Max
1994, 85 min. Director: Julien Temple. Cast: The Rolling Stones. The "world's greatest rock and roll band" prove they can still pack an arena.

From

Armst

"It's slightly ironic that tonight we're all here . . . on our best behavior, but that we're being rewarded for 25

The Hall of Fame Inductees

to

rong

of bad behavior."—Mick Jagger, 1989

Zappa:

Leaders in the music industry joined together in 1983 to establish the Rock and Roll Hall of Fame Foundation. One of the Foundation's many goals and functions is to recognize the contributions of those who have had a significant impact over the evolution, development and perpetuation of rock and roll, by inducting them into the Hall of Fame.

There are three categories of inductees:

Performers: Artists become eligible for induction twenty-five years after the release of their first record.

Non-Performers: Songwriters, producers, disc jockeys, record executives, journalists and others who had an impact on the development of rock and roll.

Early Influences: Artists whose music predated rock and roll, but who inspired rock's leading artists and helped in the evolution of rock.

The Foundation's nominating committee, composed of rock and roll historians, selects nominees each year in the Performer category. Ballots are sent to an international voting body of about 1,000 rock experts. Those performers who receive the highest number of votes, and more than 50% of the vote, are inducted. The Foundation generally inducts five to seven performers each year.

The nominating committee annually elects the inductees in the Non-Performer and Early Influence categories.

Overheard at the Induction Ceremonies

"I met Dick when I was seventeen, and at that time I looked up to him like a father. Then I got a little older. In the seventies I started regarding him as a brother. These days I look at him as a son."–Dion on Dick Clark, 1993

"We had sort of a lot of rivalry in those early years and a little bit of friction, but we always ended up friends and I'd like to think we still are."–Mick Jagger on the Beatles, 1988

"More than any other group that ever was, the Who were our role models. I love them and hate them for that."–Bono, 1990

1986

Chuck Berry
James Brown
Ray Charles
Sam Cooke
Fats Domino
The Everly Brothers
Buddy Holly
Jerry Lee Lewis
Elvis Presley
Little Richard

Non-Performers
Alan Freed
Sam Phillips

Early Influences
Robert Johnson
Jimmie Rodgers
Jimmy Yancey

Lifetime Achievement
John Hammond

1987

The Coasters
Eddie Cochran
Bo Diddley
Aretha Franklin
Marvin Gaye
Bill Haley
B. B. King
Clyde McPhatter
Rick Nelson
Roy Orbison

Carl Perkins
Smokey Robinson
Big Joe Turner
Muddy Waters
Jackie Wilson

Non-Performers
Leonard Chess
Ahmet Ertegun
Jerry Leiber and Mike Stoller
Jerry Wexler

Early Influences
Louis Jordan
T-Bone Walker
Hank Williams

1988
The Beach Boys
The Beatles
The Drifters
Bob Dylan
The Supremes

Non-Performer
Berry Gordy

Early Influences
Woody Guthrie
Lead Belly
Les Paul

"A lot of people thought that Rod and I had a love-hate relationship. That is true. He loves me and I hate him."–Jeff Beck on Rod Stewart, 1994

"I love this band because they had no limits. They weren't musical snobs and never held on to any one style. I want to tell [them] that we and millions of fans all over the world hold them in the highest esteem." –Joe Perry (Aerosmith) on Led Zeppelin, 1995

"I went to visit the Band in Woodstock, and I really sort of went there to ask if I could join the group. Only I didn't have the guts to say it."–Eric Clapton, 1994

"This band were geniuses, they still are. They made me love America so much more because they existed." –Elton John on the Beach Boys, 1988

"The way that Elvis freed your body, Bob freed your mind."
–Bruce Springsteen on Bob Dylan

"Can anyone imagine what the last twenty-five years of American popular music would be without Stevie Wonder? He is the composer of his generation."
–Paul Simon, 1989

"In their world–the Motown and soul world–they were like the Beatles. They were the most flamboyant. They had the best harmonies and they were the best live performers of all the Motown acts."
–Daryl Hall on the Temptations, 1989

1989
Dion
Otis Redding
The Rolling Stones
The Temptations
Stevie Wonder

Non-Performer
Phil Spector

Early Influences
The Ink Spots
Bessie Smith
The Soul Stirrers

1990
Hank Ballard
Bobby Darin
The Four Seasons
The Four Tops
The Kinks
The Platters
Simon and Garfunkel
The Who

Non-Performers
Gerry Goffin and Carole King
Holland, Dozier and Holland

Early Influences
Louis Armstrong
Charlie Christian
Ma Rainey

1991

LaVern Baker
The Byrds
John Lee Hooker
The Impressions
Wilson Pickett
Jimmy Reed
Ike and Tina Turner

Non-Performers
Dave Bartholomew
Ralph Bass

Early Influence
Howlin' Wolf

Lifetime Achievement
Nesuhi Ertegun

1992

Bobby "Blue" Bland
Booker T. and the MGs
Johnny Cash
Jimi Hendrix Experience
Isley Brothers
Sam and Dave
The Yardbirds

Non-Performers
Leo Fender
Bill Graham
Doc Pomus

Early Influences
Elmore James
Professor Longhair

"Janis Joplin was the sixties. She was the style, the sound, the inspiration for women and men all over the world. She was the passion and power of love–and of freedom." –Melissa Etheridge, 1995
"In the tradition of the great Irish poets and the great soul singers, he is the Caruso of rock and roll."–Robbie Robertson on Van Morrison, 1993
"I guess I've copied more licks off Les than anybody else." –Jeff Beck on Les Paul, 1988
"I love them so much because they remind me of myself. They dress like me." –Little Richard on the Supremes, 1988
"I heard a band possessed by the moment, reveling in the joys of being pissed off."–Dave Pirner (Soul Asylum) on the Animals, 1994

"It was something very special that came from America. Duane Eddy. Duane. I'd never heard that name before when I was a kid. What is that? Is that a name or is that some tank or something?"
–Mick Jones (Foreigner), 1994
"A great songwriter, a great performer, a great Canadian."
–Eddie Vedder on Neil Young, 1995
"They gave us the word. And the word was this: Don't just stay in the house and stare at the ceiling. Go up on the roof and look at the stars."–Billy Joel on the Drifters, 1988

1993
Ruth Brown
Cream
Creedence Clearwater Revival
The Doors
Etta James
Frankie Lymon and the Teenagers
Van Morrison
Sly and the Family Stone

Non-Performers
Dick Clark
Milt Gabler

Early Influence
Dinah Washington

1994
The Animals
The Band
Duane Eddy
The Grateful Dead
Elton John
John Lennon
Bob Marley
Rod Stewart

Non-Performer
Johnny Otis

Early Influence
Willie Dixon

1995
The Allman Brothers Band
Al Green
Janis Joplin
Led Zeppelin
Martha and the Vandellas
Neil Young
Frank Zappa

Non-Performer
Paul Ackerman

Early Influence
The Orioles

1996
David Bowie
Gladys Knight and the Pips
Jefferson Airplane
Little Willie John
Pink Floyd
The Shirelles
The Velvet Underground

Non-Performer
Tom Donahue

Early Influence
Pete Seeger

"Etta James is one of the few vocalists who sings truth into every note . . . for a song cannot be sung until its singer has learned and has a grip on both its freedom and its cage." –k.d.lang, 1993 "The one thing I always wanted to see–like most people want to see the Beatles back together– is Sly and the Family Stone just standing somewhere in the same room." –George Clinton, 1993 "I'm really an absolute stone fan of the Stones, and always have been. Their early shows were just shocking, absolutely riveting and stunning and moving and they changed my life completely. . . . Whatever you do, don't try to grow old gracefully. It wouldn't suit you."–Pete Town- shend on the Rolling Stones, 1989